What is Empathy

2 Books

Introducing Emotional Intelligence

Empathy

Introducing
EMOTIONAL INTELLIGENCE

COPYRIGHT © 2021. ALL RIGHTS RESERVED.

No part of this publication may be reproduced, distributed, or transmitted in any form or by any means, including photocopying, recording, or other electronic or mechanical methods, or by any information storage and retrieval system without the prior written permission of the publisher, except in the case of very brief quotations embodied in critical reviews and certain other noncommercial uses permitted by copyright law.

TABLE OF CONTENTS

INTRODUCTION

EMOTIONAL INTELLIGENCE

EMOTION AND INTELLIGENCE

CRUSHING STRESS WITH EMOTIONAL INTELLIGENCE

ROLE OF EMPATHY IN LIFE

EMOTIONAL MATURITY AND EMOTIONAL INTELLIGENCE

FUNDAMENTALS OF EMOTIONAL INTELLIGENCE

EMPATHY VS EMOTIONAL INTELLIGENCE

WHY IS EMOTIONAL INTELLIGENCE IMPORTANT?

IMPROVING YOUR LEVEL OF EMOTIONAL INTELLIGENCE

TYPES OF EMOTIONAL INTELLIGENCE

BENEFIT OF EMOTIONAL INTELLIGENCE

EMOTIONAL INTELLIGENCE FOR LEADERS

LEADERSHIP LIFESTYLE TO EMULATE

LOW EMOTIONAL CAPABILITIES CAN RUIN YOU

EI FOR THE SALESMAN

12 ELEMENTS OF EMOTIONAL INTELLIGENCE

EMOTIONAL INTELLIGENCE IN THE HOME: RAISING EMOTIONALLY INTELLIGENT CHILDREN

UNDERSTANDING THE EMOTIONS OF OTHERS

EMOTIONAL INTELLIGENCE AND SELF-ESTEEM

HOW TO USE THE ABCDE THEORY OF EMOTIONS

MASTERY OF EMOTION: A KEY TO A BETTER LIFE

GROWING EMOTIONAL INTELLIGENCE

CONCLUSION

INTRODUCTION

Emotional intelligence has a lot to do with being intelligent, and intelligence is a skill that can be developed upon, man is an emotional being and emotional beings are individuals with feelings, complex feelings as a result of the many happenings that occur on day to day basis can create various issues for humans and how they relate with people, emotional intelligence helps individuals come to grip with this inborn ability that we have been created with and helps us to understand humans around us. Through empathy people can place themselves in the experiences of others and understand how they are feeling. Using skills like self-awareness, self-motivation individuals can improve on their emotional illiteracy and be more aware of themselves, to attain mastery of emotions you would need to take cognizance of your character. Emotional intelligent people are great masters of emotions, they are individuals who are masters at communication, leading teams and learning from mistakes, they are not selfish and through the course of this book we would take time to explain how to achieve emotional intelligence for leaders, at the workplace and at the home how parents can raise emotional children. We would come to understand that lack of adequate emotional intelligence can be a barrier to growth and the attainment of success.

We use our emotions to control how we react to situations and is therefore a major factor in determining our personality, who we are. The number of definitions as to what emotional intelligence really is are, of course, far too many and complex for this short article however, what we can confirm is that there are two constants in all this. Firstly, the concept of what emotions are and secondly, understanding the context of emotions.

Today we can clearly see that being only "book smart" and having a high intelligence quotient or IQ does not guarantee a successful, happy and fulfilled life. There are many people in all parts of the world who are very brilliant academically but are inept at dealing with people and successful at work or in their personal relationships. Academic intelligence is not enough on its own to be successful in life. IQ can help you get a job and earn a living, but it does not show you how to live a life. When it comes to happiness and success in life, emotional intelligence helps you build stronger relationships, succeed at work, and achieve your career and personal goals.

Emotionally intelligent people are able to recognize their own emotional state and the emotional states of others and as a result they connect more easily with people. They therefore communicate better, form stronger relationships, achieve greater success at work, and lead a more fulfilling life. John Gottman was right when he said "In the last decade or so, science has discovered a tremendous amount about the role emotions play in our lives. Researchers have found that even more than IQ, your emotional awareness and abilities to handle feelings will determine your success and happiness in all walks of life, including family relationships."

Our natural state of being, as one with Soul, is a harmonious state of Love, in which the only feelings are of continuous peace and bliss. Therefore if we are feeling any feeling other than peace and bliss, we have got out of balance somewhere. This is due to our conditioned and faulty thinking, which emerges as tolerations, needs and limiting beliefs. Using our Emotional Intelligence equips us to identify the message that Soul is sending us through these feelings, so we can rectify our thinking and thus move always towards Love.

Being Emotionally Intelligent is my ability to consciously comprehend my own emotional States of Being. Being 'Emotional' means that I am aware of the feeling that is my emotional state of being. Being 'Intelligent' means I have a rational knowledge or logical understanding of the situation, occurrence and circumstances that I am currently experiencing. I am Intelligent when I can consciously rationalize what is happening in my reality. I am Emotional when I can feel the awareness of my energetic state of being - my emotional energy.

Emotional Intelligence loses clarity when I confuse 'being emotional' with 'being irrational'. When I am studying negative states of being that cause me to sub-consciously react, I am learning about my own irrational behavior that is without emotional intelligence. I am studying 'irrational intelligence'.

Being emotional is not reacting irrationally; it is being consciously-aware of my emotional state of being. I never react emotionally because with emotional intelligence I am always able to respond intelligently. Negative emotional states of being are irrational because a rationally intelligent person who is emotionally aware (intelligent) would never choose to experience them. Understanding irrational behavior does require emotional intelligence but it is not the definition of Emotional Intelligence. The true test of my Emotional Intelligence is whether I can be Happy & Well as a result of my conscious choice to be so. It is only my emotional ignorance that is depriving me of the happiness and well-being that is my true nature.

Happiness is an emotional feeling. How can a rational man be happy in a state of being disconnected and unemotional? Well-being is an emotional feeling. How can I feel well in a society that medicates physical and mental illness without one iota of emotional intelligence?

Having sympathy for other people doesn't mean anything unless I have defined the compassion that I am feeling. Defining compassion as: "Wanting to relieve the suffering of others", is a rationally intelligent definition of a physical desire not the explanation of an emotional feeling.

It is my lack of emotional intelligence that disconnects me from my true emotional nature. A analytical world has become a world that is devoid of lasting and Happiness, and a world filled with sadness and sickness. We seem to have lost our connection to our true Wealth and our true Health when, as a society, we are divided from our Emotional Intelligence.

Emotional States Of Being

Professional on the study of emotions have claimed that about 90% of emotional information that we feel is transmitted through non verbal means, by tone, gesture and glance and that we are rarely consciously awake of how much we are transmitting or reading from others.

To have to deny, to lie about, to suppress feelings, or to be blind to the feelings of others causes tensions and anxieties that limit us in our ability to connect to and live with others. It is needful that we develop emotional intelligence because the ability to move easily and interact freely in the emotional world is a very important part of what it requires to live an true and happy life on earth.

Emotional 'States of Being' require definition before I can understand them intelligently. When I define an emotional state of being, I give it definition, it becomes a definite emotion, and I become consciously-aware of its existence.

It is my conscious-awareness of the definite nature of my emotions that allows me to be emotionally intelligent.

An 'Emotional' person is aware of their feelings as different emotions.

An 'Emotionally Intelligent' person is a person who is able to consciously define their emotional state of being and create it at will, if and when they so choose. By intelligently defining an emotion, I become both emotionally aware of the feeling and rationally conscious of its definition. I cannot experience a definite emotion unless I am able to define it accurately. In the absence of naming an emotion, it will remain either a positive or a negative experience, dependent on the beliefs that I hold in my sub-conscious.

I have defined emotion (emotional state of being) with an adjective, which is a describing word. Any adjective that describes my feelings or my emotional state of being is an emotion. Without an adjective to describe it and name the expression, an emotion is just a feeling that is really hard to understand. One should not feel that Being emotional is reacting irrationally; it is being mentally-aware of my emotional state of being. I never react emotionally because with emotional intelligence I know how to respond intelligently during situations that call for response. Negative emotional states of being are irrational because a rationally intelligent person who is emotionally conscious (intelligent) would not choose to experience them, they are just not good for you. Understanding irrational behaviour does require emotional intelligence but it is not the definition of Emotional Intelligence.

The Potential Of My Emotional Energy

Emotion is an energetic state of being that I am experiencing. All forms of energy have a force, a magnitude and a potential. Emotions are no different. The potential of any energy is realized when the force and magnitude of that energy unite.

Electrical energy has a force called 'volts', a magnitude called 'amps' and a potential called 'watts'. They are all named after the person who first defined them. Emotional energy is more complicated because not only is its potential divided by force and magnitude but its force is divided by polarity and its magnitude is divided by gender.

The polarity of my emotions is either positive or negative and the gender of my energy is either male or female. (Anger & pride are male whereas meekness & humility are female. However, Impatience and intolerance are usually seen as negative and patience and tolerance as positive).

The degree, to which my emotional energy is unbalanced, by being divided by either polarity or gender or both, determines the intensity of the emotion that I am feeling. The greater is the imbalance the greater is the intensity of the emotional feeling. The intensity of my emotional state of being is the product of both the gender and the polarity of the emotional energy.

Emotional Intelligence requires not only the definition of my emotional state of being but the understanding of its potential for my Life.

Understanding the potential of my emotional energy requires me to be consciously-aware of:

- Its force and magnitude
- Its gender, polarity and intensity
- Its definition or Adjectivity
- The sponsoring thought or thoughts that are creating the emotion.

The Ultimate Potential of my Emotional Energy is the Pure Feeling of Love that emanates from my Soul.

Life is an emotional experience.

My Emotional Intelligence requires more than my ability to manage my irrational behavior. It requires the ability to understand my emotional experiences intelligently. The cause of my irrational behavior is my lack of emotional intelligence. I react irrationally with what is sometimes confusingly called an emotional reaction.

I respond with positive emotion once I attain the intelligence and understanding to do so. My symptoms of irrational behavior are created by my lack of rational intelligence. Extreme irrational behavior caused by a lack of rational ability may be diagnosed as a mental illness by a rational person who has no emotional intelligence.

Diagnosing emotional disorder or disease requires emotional intelligence not rational intelligence, which is probably why illness is usually diagnosed as either physical or mental and not emotional. In the absence of emotional intelligence, my life became an unemotional experience as a rationally intelligent man.

In a dualistic world, the more rationally intelligent I become the more contained, disconnected and emotionally unintelligent I am. It is my experience that the more I rationalize my world with tolerance and patience the less I react with the frustration of my anger and intolerance. However, with emotional intelligence I consciously choose to be 'Accepting' instead of tolerant and I choose to be 'Allowing' instead of patient. I no longer choose to be a tolerant patient who is patiently tolerating Life.

I have decided to accept that Life as an emotional experience because I am learning to be emotionally intelligent enough to see it that way.

EMOTIONAL INTELLIGENCE

Emotional intelligence which stands for EI, is the unlearned attribute humans have to detect, assess, and affect their own emotion and the emotions of other people in their immediate environment. This concept of emotional intelligence itself started with Dr. Wayne Payne in the year 1985, but emotional intelligence became popular when the author Daniel Goldman came up with a book on Emotional Intelligence , EI also refers to the an individual's ability to identify and manage one's own emotions, as well as the emotions of others. Though there is some disagreement within the circle of psychologists as to what constitutes true emotional intelligence, it is generally said to include at least three skills: emotional awareness, or the ability to identify and name one's own emotions; the ability to harness those emotions and apply them to tasks like thinking and problem solving; and the ability to manage emotions, which includes both regulating one's own emotions when necessary and cheering up or calming down other people.

Emotional intelligence can also be defined as that in born natural ability to recognize and understand emotions in yourself and others, and your ability to use this knowledge to manage your person, relationships and relationships around you. Emotional intelligence is the "something" in each of us that is a bit abstract. It affects how we manage behavior, how we meander through social complexities, and make individual decisions in one's life so as to achieve positive results in life's endeavors. This ability called emotional intelligence taps into a key element of human behavior that is distinct from your intellect. There is no known connection between IQ and EQ; you simply can't predict EQ based on how smart someone is. Cognitive intelligence, or IQ, is not flexible. Your IQ except in the case of traumatic event such as a brain injury remains the same from birth. You don' t get smarter by learning new facts or information. Intelligence is your ability to learn, and it's the same at age 10 as it is at age 40. EQ, on the other hand, is a flexible skill that can be groomed. While it is true that some people are naturally more emotionally intelligent than others, a high EQ can be improved upon even if you aren't born with it.

There is currently no validated measurement or scale for emotional intelligence as there is for "g," the general intelligence factor, a fact that has led some critics to claim the concept is either a myth or entirely non-existent. Despite this criticism, however, emotional intelligence (or "emotional quotient," as its sometimes known) has wide appeal among the general public, as well as in certain industries. In recent years, some employers have even incorporated "emotional intelligence tests" into their application or interview processes, on the theory that someone high in emotional intelligence would make a better leader or coworker. But while some studies have found a link between emotional intelligence and job performance, others have shown no correlation, and the lack of a scientifically valid scale makes it difficult to truly measure or predict someone's emotional intelligence on the job.

Identifying individuals who have high EQ is usually very easy. They are very self-aware people and they take their time to reflect on their actions and emotions. They recognize what triggers certain emotions and how to handle them even under desperate circumstances. They also know when they may have reached a "boiling point" and need to cool down or take some steam off the situation for a while; they evaluate the situation of things and come up a solution. It is like hitting the pause button on a remote control.

Studies in the early 1990's by John Mayer and Peter Salovey came up with a working model of emotional intelligence that defined it as the capacity to understand and to reason with emotions. In their analysis, Mayer and Salovey, broke emotional intelligence down into four parts:

Self-Awareness: this is the ability and need to understand your own emotions, knowing what those emotions are, and acknowledging those feelings. Self-empathy is the act of giving ourselves empathy, listening to our own feelings and unmet needs with compassion and understanding. This does not make the problems go away, or magically make all our needs met. But it does help us to feel connected and centered within ourselves. It can also be a tool to express ourselves with more honesty. Though it doesn't make problems go away, it makes it easier to endure them. It is that natural ability to know which emotions you are experiencing and the reason why you feel that way. When you understand your emotions, it is easier for you to understand, accept and control your emotions and avoid your feelings from controling you. You also become more confident, and bold as you do not let your emotions get out of control. Being self-aware also enables you to take an sincere stance at yourself, be honest with yourself so you can improve on your strengths and know what your weaknesses are, and work on these areas to achieve better outcomes for yourself and others.

You can start to look at Self-Awareness as setting the starting point for your life. For that reason, it is as an essential starting place from which you build the other important aspects of your life. Although Self-Awareness embraces many things, being concious of your own emotions and feelings should be the first and most vital step to take to becoming Emotionally Intelligent. We undergo many different feelings and emotions on a daily basis. These two words (feelings and emotions) are sometimes used interchangeably, but they have different meanings. If we understand the differences, it can greatly shape us into becoming more self-aware about ourselves.

Self-awareness is the foundational competency of the Emotional Intelligence (EI) model and I have made researches and worked on this topic for more than a decade now. This competency provides a solid base upon which to build and enhance Emotional Intelligence competencies including emotional self-management, emotional self-motivation, and empathy and nurturing relationships. Yet many of us go through our day unaware and very accepting of the emotional roller coaster daily events evoke. Without recognizing where we are expanding our emotional energy, it has now become very hard to progress to developing other EI abilities.

Self-Motivation: this is the ability to remain focused on a goal despite your level of self-doubt and impulsiveness. It means feeling physically along with the other person as though their emotions are contagious. It makes one well-attuned to another's emotional world, which is a plus in any of the wide range of callings. There is a downside attached to emotional empathy that occurs, when people lack the ability to manage their own emotions.

This can be seen as psychological exhaustion leading to a burnout as commonly seen in professionals. The purposeful detachment cultivated by those in medical profession is a way to void burnout. But when the detachment leads to indifference, it can seriously hamper the professional care.

Individuals who are self-motivated are always eager to take on difficult tasks and challenges, they are self-assured people and are very energetic internally, they are also very good at raising thier voice towards unpopular opinions, they are decisive and resilient.

Empathy: the ability to tune into the feelings of others and effectively understanding them pretty much the same way as they understand themselves. A type of empathy called Cognitive empathy that is the ability to handle emotions in a mature way that is relevant to the present situation. It means knowing how the other person feels and what they might be thinking. It is very helpful in negotiations or motivating people. It has been found that people who possess good cognitive empathy (also called perspective taking) make good leaders or managers because they are able to move people to give their best efforts. But there can be a downside to this type of empathy. If people, falling within the "Dark Triad" - narcissists, Machiavellians and psychopaths - possess ample ability of cognitive empathy, they can exploit others to the extent of torturing them. Such people have no sympathy for their victims and expertly use their ability to carry out their cruelty.

Empathy is very present in humans to many degrees of extents and, therefore, we are affected by the other person's predicament in a different way. In fact, it is one of the first traits of humans so much so that any individual lacking of this ability is seen as not ok, seen as mentally ill or dangerous. From tests carried out and observation Females most times score higher on standard tests of empathy, social sensitivity, and emotion recognition than do males. Its inherence in humans can be proven by the fact that young children respond to the emotions of family members even from that early age, this is proof that its an innate ability. Besides kids, Some domestic animals have also express their worry, when the family members are in distress. There has been reports of dogs rescuing injured persons from fire or detecting sadness. Some pets would stay around and place their heads in their owners' laps , making sounds, and this shows that even animals have empathy. Besides humans, many other species exhibit presence of empathy to a varying extent. Like dolphins who have rescued people on countless occasions and saved people from shark attacks.

A good case scenario for validating the presence of empathy in animals came from these research. The researchers reported in 1964 in the American Journal of Psychiatry that Rhesus monkeys refused to pull a chain that dispatched food to themselves if doing so gave a shock to a companion.one of the monkies stopped pulling the chain for 12 days after witnessing another monkey receive a shock. These primates were literally starving themselves in order to avoid causing harm to one another. We can express empathy through statements such as, "I can see you not very comfortable with this and it doesnt sit well with you," and "I can can see why you are very upset about this issue." We can show empathy through a hug, a pat on the back, body contact, a touch, and even through a "high five to boost morale" when our empathy relates to someone's success. Empathy is not the same emotion as sympathy. Where empathy allows us to vicariously experience and identify with other's feelings, sympathy is a feeling of pity or sorrow for the feelings of others. With empathy we feel with someone else, with sympathy we feel for someone else.

There are many theories concerning the nature versus nurture aspect of empathic development. Are some people born virtuous and some people born evil? Dr. Paul Zak has studied the biological basis of good versus evil behavior over a number of years and has made a very interesting discovery. He found that when people feel for other people, the stress triggers the brain to release a chemical called oxytocin. Likewise, a study at Berkely concluded that a particular variant of the oxytocin receptor gene is associated with the trait of human empathy. In the study, those who had this gene variant were found to have a more empathic nature. Dr. Zak says that this study demonstrates that some people, about five percent of our population, may have a gene variant that makes them less empathic. In other words, he says, some people are more or less immune to oxytocin.

So there is scientific evidence that the goodness trait is encoded in our genes. But nature is not the only influencing factor. We may be born with the capacity to have empathy, but our ability to apply it, to care and understand, is a learned behavior.

Social psychologists say that empathetic behavior is built from the secure attachment babies develop with their parents or primary caregivers, and by modeling their parents' empathetic behavior towards them and others. Sincere empathetic behavior develops in children whose parents constantly show, teach, and reinforce it. It is a gradual emergence that occurs with the consistency and caring shown to them during the formative years of their social and emotional development. In many cases, but not all, adults who lack empathy have been victims of childhood abuse or neglect.

Those who have had extremely painful childhoods, ones that have involved emotional, sexual, or physical abuse, often lose touch with their own feelings while shutting themselves off from the pain. Their underdeveloped coping skills leave them saddled with distress, whether their own or others, and their lack of ability to experience their own pain prevents them from feeling the pain of others. As adults their elaborately built defense mechanisms block guilt and shame while also blocking their conscience. They live life through fear, threats, punishment, and isolation rather than empathy and kindness.

In many cases the opposite is true-the person over-identifies with others' pain, is overwhelmed by it, and becomes overly empathetic to the point that they absorb the feelings of everyone around them. Their internal pain and suffering is triggered when they see others in pain and suffering, therefore become preoccupied with everyone else's pain and make it their own. I did that for most of my life. Often it was to deflect my own pain but ironically it caused me to suffer more. I had very poor coping skills and my boundaries were out of whack if existent at all. I also modeled the behavior I observed as a child.

I do think that overall, my generation, a generation that relied on human interaction, a generation where families visited relatives and friends every

Sunday because there was nothing else to do, is more empathetic than the generations that have followed.

In fact, an eye opening new study presented by University of Michigan researchers at an Association for psychological science annual meeting claims that college students who started school after the year 2000 have empathy levels that are 40% lower than students thirty years prior. The sharpest drop occurred in the last nine years. The study includes data from over 14,000 students.

One reason that this is happening is because students are becoming more self-oriented as their world becomes increasingly more competitive. Some say that social networking is creating a more narcissistic generation. According to lead researchers, it is harder for today's college student to empathize with others because so much of their social interactions are done through a computer or cell phone and not through real life interaction. With their friends online they can pick and choose who they will respond to and who they will tune out. That is more than likely to carry over into real life.

This is also a generation that grew up playing video games. Much of their formative years development has been influenced by input from computer generated images and violent cyber-interactions. There has to be a connection. This may partly explain the numbing of this generation. Another point of view was presented by Christopher Lasch, a renowned and popular American historian, moralist, and social critic, in a book he published in 1979 called, The Culture of Narcissism: American Life in an Age of Diminishing Expectations. Lasch links the prevalence of narcissism in our society to the decline of the family unit, loss of core values, and long-term social disintegration in the twentieth century.

He believed that the liberal, utopian lifestyle of the 60's gave way to a search for personal growth in the 70's. But people were unsuccessful in their attempts to find their selves. So a movement began to build a society that celebrated self-expression, self-esteem, and self-love. That's all well and good, or so it seems, but as a result of the "me" focus, more narcissism was inadvertently created. It all backfired-aggression, materialism, lack of caring for others, and shallow values have been the result.

There are certainly many of us who have not become this way-studies speak for society in general. Today we live with constant internal and external pressures of life. On a daily basis our society faces terrorism, crime, economic crises, widespread job insecurity, war, political corruption. We see the disintegration of morality wherever we look.

As a writer, author, and inspirer I was greatly disturbed by the overwhelming success of a book (I will not promote the name except to say that it has the word "gray" in the title) based on pornography and smut. It astounds me that millions of people have read it. If I were the publisher I would have instantly rejected a manuscript of such low moral content and offensive subject matter. Where has our appreciation for quality literature as a society gone to? And what has happened to our legal system? It has been demonstrated time and time again that the rights of the innocent take a back seat to the rights of the offender. Our laws do very little to control criminals. In fact, it seems as if criminals control the law. If ever an empathy disorder could spur unthinkable violence to erupt in a seemingly normal person, now is the time.

Emotional intelligence is learned through experience, reflection and modeling over a long period of time. Time must be set aside with someone you trust and respect that will allow you to experiment with and practice new behaviors, thoughts and feelings to the point of mastery. The environment needs to be supportive, emotionally engaging and offer time for practice.

If you are really interested in increasing your Self-Awareness, the following steps are necessary:

1. Acknowledge the fact that self-improvement is very vital.

2. Know the kind of person you want to be.

3. Realize your strengths, weakness and limitations as well as your values. Know what you stand for.

4. Find out about what people think of you, get feedback from people - who do people say you are , how you are perceived by others can be used to determine the gap between who you want to be and who you are presently.

5. Work with a supportive groups, encouraging people you trust (a coach is ideal) who can guide, teaches you and hold you accountable as you experiment with new thoughts, feelings and behavior in order to build on your strengths.

6. Put them into pracice , try out the new behaviors over time until your ideal self is realized. Increasing the three areas of Self-Awareness is worth the effort. It establishes the foundation upon which to build relationships and handle the challenges in your personal and professional life.

EMOTION AND INTELLIGENCE

Emotions and intelligence are indispensable terms and would be discussed throughout the length of this book. An understanding of these terms is important for an ensuing comprehension of EI (Alston, 2009). The Oxford English Dictionary defined emotion as "any agitation or disturbance of mind, feeling, passion; any vehement or excited mental state". Emotion is a neutral way to look at feelings, on the surface we can call emotions feeling. Among the circle of psychologists the definitions of emotions hardly varies as they all seem to agree. So, although you may feel "repelling" or weird, this is the part where a psychologist tries to detect if an emotion represents sadness, nervousness, irritability, anxiety or anger.

It is very easy to remember the difference between emotions and feelings with this idea: Emotions are the objective state of feelings. Emotions are clear, well-defined, and experienced by all people. Over the year Psychologists have identified several types of emotions that that has been expressed by humans. What they discovered is that you can also have a variety of emotions. A very good example to understanding what I mean by various types of emotions is when you think of mixing various ingredients or condiments together in the kitchen, when you combine flour, milk, vinegar and eggs, and then heat the mixture to make a pie. Now this is how two expressions of emotions can combine together, sometimes it might get a little complicated .Like how annoyance and irritation can combine to create rage if you don't check those emotions. Joy and excitement can lead to optimism. Feelings are the more prejudiced aspects of emotions, feelings can be hard to interpret. Some people are better at identifying their feelings than others are. You may find feelings less clear than emotions. For example, Julia overhears a co-worker telling someone that

Ted just got the job promotion Julia had applied for. She had been so sure that she was next in line for the job. As soon as she hears the news, Julia has a queasy, upset feeling in her stomach. She says she feels bloated, probably from something she ate. Although she believes she's feeling queasy — at least, that's her subjective experience — an outside observer could probably figure out that she really feels a bit traumatized and depressed. Now thats a narraive , another angle to look at it is that sometimes emotions overpower us because we draw them out of proportion we, make it seem bigger than usual. And this is what pessimistic thinkers do. They extend the negative emotion into broad areas of their lives. This is the quintessential "bring the office home" individual. I knew one executive who allowed anger at work to pervade all areas of his life.

Life happens. Events take place that are beyond our control, and some of them can be extremely upsetting and all-consuming. We can't avoid negative situations, nor can we change the behavior or opinions of other people involved. We can only look honestly at our own reactions and try to channel our responses into a positive direction.

Emotional balance is achieved through identifying, feeling and processing our emotional reactions in appropriate and healthy ways.

Here are some strategies to re-shape your reactions and find relief.

1. Briefly summarize the situation. Try to state what's happened as simply and unemotionally as possible, using concise and neutral language. Reducing your problem to its simplest form is a great way of making it seem smaller and more manageable.

For example, your mind may be screaming: "I can't believe she betrayed my trust! Why would she blab something I told her in strict confidence? She promised she wouldn't tell anyone. Now everyone is going to know! I'll never trust her again.

A simpler, calmer description would be: "I shared a secret with a friend who told it to someone else."

Restating the problem succinctly and neutrally takes away a lot of its drama and power. It also makes the situation seem less personal and unique. Lots of people fail to keep secrets and the world keeps turning. You can survive this.

2. Describe your current reaction to your challenge. How do you truly feel at this moment? Don't hold back. Are you angry, fearful, regretful, anxious, overwhelmed, defeated, resentful, or agitated? Get in touch with your true feelings. Acknowledge them; they belong to you and they are real.

3. Create a rating system (numbers, stars, plus signs, exclamation marks, etc.) and evaluate the intensity of your reaction. This is a form of validation and a way to judge where you are along the path of emotional healing.

4. Envision your desired emotional reaction. What's your concept of a healthy and appropriate response? How do you want to handle this situation? What kind of genuine reaction would make you feel like you handled yourself with dignity, fairness and grace?

5. Think about actions you can take to move closer to your desired reaction. For example, you may think you owe someone an apology, even though you might not be ready to make it at this time.

Look at what role you played in creating the current situation. Do you need to change your attitude or perspective? Make the situation less personal or important? Or do you need to simply do nothing until a desirable course of action becomes clearer?

You may need to repeat these steps a number of times before you experience a calmer, more serene response. Keeping a journal may help you gain insight and see progress. Hopefully, with repetition and persistence you will streamline your path towards peace and emotional balance.

CRUSHING STRESS WITH EMOTIONAL INTELLIGENCE

Work stress is as old as work itself and so are the ways we respond. You can just imagine the first cave-clan's leader spending sleepless nights counting stalactites, worried about how he was going to break the news to UG and the other hunters that the decreasing wild beast population meant they were going to have less to eat.

Stress always has, and probably always will, go hand-in-hand with work.

Unfortunately, stress appears to be on the rise. In a study conducted earlier this year at the University of Rochester Medical Center in New York, Dr. Diana Fernandez, MD, found that job stress not only makes workers unhappier but also harms their health. In her study of 2,782 employees at a large manufacturing facility, Fernandez and her team found strong links between job stress and cardiovascular disease, depression, exhaustion, and weight gain. After a tense day of pink slips circulating around the office, many workers told Fernandez's team that they looked forward to going home and "vegging out" in front of the TV. In the American Psychological Association's 2009 Stress in America Survey, 42% of Americans said their stress levels had increased since the previous year. A lukewarm economy and high unemployment suggest that 2011's numbers aren't going to improve.

But what if you could reduce stress without having to wait for the economy to improve? A promising stream of research linking emotional intelligence (EQ) to stress-reduction offers exciting new clues about how to beat stress in spite of economic woes.

A team of Belgian researchers led by Dr. Moira Mikolajczak found that levels of emotional intelligence-a person's ability to understand and manage his or her own emotions and those of other people-determine how effectively people cope with stress. Mikolajczak found that people with high emotional intelligence report better moods, less anxiety, and less worry during times of tension and stress than those with less ability to identify and manage their emotions.

But emotional intelligence is not just about naïve optimism or disguising negative emotions by forcing yourself to put on a happy face. Emotionally intelligent people actually feel less stress. Emotionally intelligent people have improved their ability to engage their emotions and rational thinking simultaneously. This results in a more contained, comfortable reaction to stressful circumstances. As your EQ increases, you actually feel less stress. Without consciously trying to control their reactions to stress, high EQ individuals show fewer physical signs of stress reactions, such as sweaty palms, elevated heart rate, and increased secretion of certain hormones and brain chemicals. When facing a situation that sends most people climbing up the walls, a high-EQ person approaches the stressor with the same calm composure that most people demonstrate only in the most trivial of circumstances.

In other words, emotionally intelligent people not only claim to experience less stress, they also physically and mentally experience less stress.

Why Emotional Intelligence Matters:

The Belgian researcher's uncovered two primary reasons for emotional intelligence limiting stress. First, they found that emotionally intelligent people evaluate their environment differently. In the words of Dr. Mikolajczak, they "are particularly inclined to look for the silver lining, invoke pleasant thoughts or memories in order to counter their current emotional state, think about what steps to take in order to handle the problem, and put it into perspective. In contrast, they seem less likely to catastrophize or to blame themselves for the occurrence of the problem and/or for their incapacity to solve it."

Second, and perhaps most important, people who are good with emotions are more likely to choose a "problem-focused" coping strategy. Each problem we encounter presents us with two choices: address the problem head-on or bury our heads in the sand, hoping that the issue will resolve itself. People who employ a problem-focused coping strategy devote their attention to solving the problem, rather than ignoring it. This adaptive approach to solving problems works to squash the cause of the stress and lessens the amount of stress experienced because the mere act of devising a plan makes you feel more relaxed and in control. People enjoy challenging jobs, crossword puzzles, and Sudoku for the same reason-solving problems is mentally stimulating.

In contrast, less emotionally intelligent people let their fear and anxiety drive them toward a "problem-avoidance" coping strategy, which only prolongs the tension. As you might guess, these two strategies become a self-fulfilling prophecy-confirming the belief that led the individual to think that way in the first place and furthering his or her conviction that the problem is too much to handle. The habit of avoiding problems doesn't make you forget them. Instead, it keeps you wallowing in the negative emotions that accompany a burdensome challenge. The problem itself remains a perpetual source of stress, amplifying the bad feelings that make stress hard to deal with.

In theory, it would seem that you could take a shortcut by skipping the emotional intelligence piece and just learning the adaptive coping strategies. The only problem is that people who aren't good with emotions are also poor at using a problem-focused strategy. Only the emotionally intelligent bunch-who know how to fend off the distractions created by fear, sadness, anger, jealousy, shame, and the like-are able to effectively implement a problem-focused approach.

EQ Training: The Gift That Keeps On Giving:

Fortunately, virtually anyone can develop emotional intelligence with training. The Belgian team proved that emotional intelligence could be significantly improved with only a handful of short training sessions. In a series of four 150-minute trainings spread out over a month, participants significantly increased their ability to identify and manage emotions. The trainings included such basic training elements as short lectures, role-playing, group discussions, reading assignments, and a daily journal entry about one emotional experience.

Most amazing, however, is that the people who received emotional intelligence training not only maintained their new emotional intelligence skills six months after the training ended but also showed a slight improvement in their EQ at the six-month follow-up. We can only imagine how much they would have improved had they received even a brief reminder to practice their emotional intelligence skills every few days.

How To Beat Your Stress:

To start reducing your stress by improving your own emotional intelligence, there are two basic steps.

1. Get an EQ education. The best way to educate yourself is with the help of a reputable, certified emotional intelligence trainer or coach. If you check with your training department, you might already have access to such a professional within your organization.

2. Practice. After you have developed the right foundation of emotional intelligence knowledge, you must practice using it. You can do this with the old-fashioned system of sticky notes on your nightstand and bathroom mirror, or you can get a little more precise with an automated reminder system.

In sum, the research you've just explored means that people-all people-are very capable of eradicating stress with a relatively small amount of emotional intelligence training. A little emotional intelligence training goes a very long way in helping you to reduce stress and handle the obstacles that life inevitable throws your way.

ROLE OF EMPATHY IN LIFE

Empathy plays great role in our life in almost every sphere. The skill of empathy, though we inherit it, can be cultivated, which plays a significant role in making us successful in those spheres. Role of empathy in the life of an individual is actually dependent on its conceptualization by the individual, which varies widely. Nevertheless, empathy acts to reflect what has been perceived and creates a supportive or confirming atmosphere. Empathy is a powerful communication skill that is actually underused by many. It allows one to understand thoughts and resultant feelings created by them in others. Empathy also makes one to respond to other's feelings sympathetically so that they can win their trust, which promotes communication further. Our fear of failure, anger, and frustration suddenly drop away, allowing for a more meaningful dialogue and a deepening of relationships.

Empathy is more than simple sympathy, which makes the individual understand others with compassion and sensitivity. That is why it is plays an important role in the workplace, where many people work together to achieve something of significance. It helps create deep respect for the co-workers, thereby fostering a harmonious atmosphere in the workplace. Similarly, empathy is helpful in our professional life because, besides facilitating communication, it makes us a sympathetic listener to our clients, whereby we are able to understand them better. Because empathy makes us able to communicate effectively and listen empathetically, we stand a better chance of making our personal and social relationships successful. In fact, empathy is capable of nurturing every kind of relationship we enter into or are in. As it is clear that empathy affects our life with far reaching ramifications, we should help our children to develop this inborn trait so that they can become better human beings for themselves and for the world. Since empathy promotes pro-social behavior, it will help our children develop close relationships, maintain friendships and develop better communities. Emotional intelligence has assumed great importance over the past twenty years as an instrument in developing an ability to work with our own and other's emotions. One of the most important components of emotional intelligence skills is empathy.

Undoubtedly, empathy immensely affects our everyday life. This trait will come in handy in situations, where we find ourselves trapped, because it will make us understand other's perspectives. While it's true that we are born with this trait and it's in unnaturally, it happens to be underused by many. As empathy is one of the most important skills to be practiced for success in everyday life, we should encourage our children to cultivate it.

Empathy is an inherent trait in humans but it is present in changeable extent in us. That is why everyone doesn't empathize to others to the same extent and in the same way. Nevertheless, it plays a significant role in our day-to-day life, contributing extensively to our personal, professional and social success.

EMOTIONAL MATURITY AND EMOTIONAL INTELLIGENCE

Emotional maturity moves beyond "intelligence" to a higher state of consciousness, guided by what one senses, feels and intuits, and one's heart.

Five principles underlie emotional maturity:

1 - Every negative emotion we experience right here and right now is actually a childhood reaction applied to a current person, circumstance or event.

2 - Most adult's are 3-4-5-year-olds in adult bodies wearing adult clothes.

3 - No one can make you feel a way you don't want to feel. You hold the power to how you want to feel.

4 - An adult can be emotionally mature and child-like or immature and child-ish.

5 - Mindfulness, focus and presence are the keys to emotional maturity.

First, emotional maturity begins with an exploration of how emotional make-up forms early on in life, based on interactions with our primary caregivers, then with extended family, teachers, friends, clergy, etc. Around seven, our psychological and emotional "programming" is set. Our reactivity (e.g., anger, sadness, fear, shame, hurt, guilt and loneliness, etc.) to people, events and circumstances that triggered us early in life is stored in our cells, and arises when "related" triggers appear later in life.

The emotionally mature adult identifies and experiences emotions without acting out, or stuffing or suppressing them. Some emotionally intelligent, but "immature," adults," knowing about emotions, are often unable to appropriately identify or manage emotions. Rather, they resort to "defended" reactivity, sidestepping their emotions: intellectualizing, explaining, analyzing, disagreeing, attacking, flattering, joking, apologizing, evading, going silent, becoming aloof or suspicious, rejecting, criticizing, judging, etc. These emotionally intelligent, but immature, folks come across as: superior, arrogant, stubborn, defiant, hostile, people-pleasing, wishy-washy, phony, resentful, intolerant, self-pitying or victimized, etc. Not mature behavior. When we explore the nature of our emotions, we move towards a "that was then; this is now" perspective, becoming less triggered by current events and circumstances. We don't "futurize" our past.

Secondly, not exploring the developmental nature of emotions, many aren't aware that childhood emotions play out in "adult" life - that we bring our "family" to our adult interactions - at work, at home, at play and in relationship. Our adult reactivity to people, places, circumstances and events that push our buttons is actually an "unconscious" reminder of childhood people, places, circumstances and events. For the emotionally immature individual their paradigm is "that was then; this is still then." Their past leaks out on to current situations.

Third. When we "work" to understand the nature of our emotions, we "get" that, as a child, we reacted the way we reacted to either feel safe and secure, or to receive acknowledgment, approval and love. The emotionally mature adult is not a child in an adult body, wearing adult clothes and does not react as a child. The emotionally mature adult understands "my emotions are not me, but mine; I'm in control, not my emotions." In this place of non-judgment, we experience an event with greater objectivly, optimally with no emotional charge or at least with less emotional charge. Emotional maturity teaches us how to detach from a person, place, and event or circumstance that would normally trigger reactivity. Here, we can remain in a state of equanimity or manageable or aware arousal. In this place, we don't choose to blame a person or thing for "making me feel" a certain way.

Fourth. Our behavior is always vacillating between the ends of two continua: (1) the child-like, emotionally mature adult and (2) the child-ish, emotionally immature adult. What do these look like? The "child-like" qualities of an emotionally-mature adult include: lively, excited, alive, juicy, adventurous, joyful, happy, open etc. The "adult" qualities of an emotionally-mature adult include: nurturing/supportive, firm/fair, helpful, respectful, self-responsible, non-judgmental, heart-felt, honest, sincere, allowing, accepting, focused on well-be-ing; one serves, coaches or mentors. On the other hand, the "child-ish" qualities of an emotionally immature adult include: reactive, acting out, throwing tantrums, fearful, scared, needy, angry, resentful, pushy, bullying, jealous, envious, shut down, quiet, withdrawn, defensive, argumentative and grandiose, etc. The "adult" qualities of an emotionally immature adult include: non-loving, overbearing, micromanaging, controlling, disrespectful, fearful, angry, negative, judgmental, critical, abusive (mentally, emotionally, psychologically, physically), dishonest, insincere, narcissistic and focused on the self and the ego. The question, "How old do I feel right now?" can support one to experience where they are on the continua in any given moment.

Fifth, The most visible and effective outcome of emotional maturity is our ability to be in the moment, in our body and present (non-reactive, non-judgmental). We track our emotions in our body. We don't "do" anything, "fix" anything, or change anything as we witness and observe our emotions rise and fall. Being present to our emotions allows our True Self (not our mind) to drive as our Heart and Soul inform us of "right knowing," "right understanding" and "right action." We have the emotion without "becoming" the emotion. We understand the "trigger" for my reactivity may be "outside" me, but the "cause" of my emotions is within. So, we watch, witness and observe as we're triggered and allow our True Self to support our inner journey and exploration, with curiosity, not efforting or mentally changing our experience. Mindfulness, presence, focus, trust and surrender to our emotional experience bring about whatever is needed in the moment. Our Heart and Soul never call for negativity or reactivity, but a considered, emotionally mature response.

In our never-ending journey of unfolding our infinite potential, emotional maturity can be thought of as a next step in the evolution of our humanity and the opening of greater, conscious awareness to our self and to others.

FUNDAMENTALS OF EMOTIONAL INTELLIGENCE

Those fundamentals include: self-awareness, self-regulation, motivation, empathy and social skills. We can spend our lives accumulating degrees, job experiences and the many certifications that we seem to need more of, but in reality, long lasting success comes from within us. Some call it wisdom. You might argue that wisdom is something that cannot be developed, it must come to us. In some cases that may be true. However, EQ or emotional intelligence can be developed and worked upon. This in turn will help us use our best thinking, and come up with the more reasonable decisions, and this in turn will help us be wiser.

Most of us have various strengths and opportunities when it comes to the building blocks of emotional intelligence. If possible, It is advisable that you take an some tests and find out how you fair compared to others. You may be surprised by the results and discover that you have strengths in areas you might not have suspected. And you may also discover that you have weak points and attributes that are holding you back from professional and personal success. However, even if you don't have the opportunity to take an assessment to learn your particularly strengths and opportunities, it can be helpful to get an understanding of the ingredients of emotional intelligence and get some ideas on how they might be strengthened.

Self-awareness as we defined earlier is the ability to recognize and understand your moods, emotions, and drives as well as understanding their effect on others. You're able to understand your limitations, strengths and emotions and then self-manage. With self-awareness, you can reduce negative leadership traits and express yourself better. You're also more likely to have higher stress tolerance and restraint. You're less likely to lose control and cause workers distress when you're frustrated or dealing with stress and/or change. This means you know how you are feeling and why. It also involves having a sense of your self-worth and your strengths. Suggestions for improving your self-awareness include. Pay serious attention to your behaviors and see if you recognize patterns throughout the day, reflect on the connection between your emotions and your behavior. Write in a journal about your emotional responses to situations that were significant. Share your introspective discoveries with a family member or trusted friend. Make a list of your strengths and areas for improvement. Look at it on a daily basis.

Self-regulation is defined as the ability to control or redirect disruptive impulses and moods and the propensity to suspend judgment and think before acting. This involves keeping your disruptive emotions and impulses in check. It involves taking personal accountability for your actions. And, it is the ability to be comfortable with new ideas, approaches, and ways of doing things. Suggestions to improving your ability to self-regulate include:

Practice self-restraint by listening first, pausing and then responding. When becoming frustrated, identify what brought on that emotion. Create effective responses to stressful situations by finding strategies for altering a negative mood. Discuss ways of dealing with change and stress with family members, friends or a trusted advisor. Focus on events that provide a sense of calm or positive emotions. Motivation as it relates to EQ is defined as a passion to work for reasons that go beyond money or status and a propensity to pursue goals with energy and persistence. This involves a readiness to act on opportunities. It also means that you are persistent in pursuing your goals despite encountering many obstacles. Ways to improve your EQ motivation include the following practices:

Set specific goals with dates for achievement. Clarify why these goals are important to you. Ask yourself not only, "What are my goals?" but also, "Why are they my goals?"

Work with a peer or trusted advisor to create detailed action items to work toward your overall goals. Set aside time to work on your goals each day, even if it is just five minutes at a time. List your goals and post them where you can see them every day.

Empathy is defined as the ability to understand the emotional make up of other people. This is your ability to sense others' feelings and perspectives and taking an active interest in their concerns. It is also the ability to cultivate opportunities through different kinds of people. It helps you anticipate, recognize and meet the needs of others. You can learn to practice more empathy by doing some of the following:

Attempt to understand others before communicating your point of view.

Observe nonverbal behavior to evaluate the negative or positive emotions of others.

Watch interactions of other people that you determine to be empathetic. What can you do to model that behavior?

Break bad interpersonal habits, such as interrupting others. Observe body language for nonverbal messages being expressed. Seek clarification from others when attempting to read emotional responses. Be nonjudgmental in your interactions with others. Social skills are a proficiency in managing relationships and building networks. These skills help you work with others toward shared goals and create group synergy in pursuing collective goals. They help you listen openly and send convincing messages, while negotiating and dissolving disagreements. You can improve your social skills by:

- ☐ Being aware of the message your body language is communicating.

- ☐ Asking those you admire to describe their experience when socializing with you.

Remembering people's names. Everyone has a hard time with it. Use memory techniques and be known as the one that remembers! After making a mistake, take accountability quickly and find ways to make amends. Taking notice when emotions are taking over an interaction and then find ways to remove yourself from the situation. Showing a genuine curiosity for others' well-being

EMPATHY VS EMOTIONAL INTELLIGENCE

Empathy is the ability to feel what the other person is feeling. It is to experience their emotions. It is the ability to put yourself in the other person's shoes in a big and meaningful way. Emotional intelligence is the ability to manage your own emotions, as well as the emotions of others. This is a skill that all great communicators possess (more about this tomorrow).Empathy and emotional intelligence work together in sales, enabled by caring, to produce long-lasting relationships. Together they are the foundation of trust.

Empathy in general would mean feeling what the other person is feeling and 'being in the shoes of the other'. Empathy creates emotional link and involvement and could be between lovers, family members, friends, or even strangers. Empathy relates to contentedness and a sense of just knowing what another person is feeling. Some individuals are simply more empathetic than others whereas some individuals could find it hard to relate. Some questions that psychology would deal with are what creates empathy and why are some individuals more empathetic than others.

Empathy or a feeling of contentedness and being in the shoes of others is closely related to intuition as intuition helps in the understanding and recognition of emotions in others. Even if emotions are covert and not manifested, empathy helps in identifying these emotions through intuition. Empathy is thus described as recognizing other people's emotions through intuition and is marked by a feeling of connecting to the other person.

In any leadership situation such as in political leadership and social leadership, it is necessary for leaders to feel certain degree of empathy with the other members of the group as the leaders have to feel connected to the followers to make an impact in their opinions and decisions. Teachers also have to feel empathy with the students as this creates a contentedness without which the teaching experience is meaningless both for the teachers and the students. Empathy is about motivating or influencing the other person by tapping in on his or her emotions. It is easier to influence or change people if you are keenly aware of what they are thinking or feeling as this helps to predict the possible responses. Finally we have understanding of other people only when we are able to predict their responses and empathy adds a predictive quality to the interaction.

Stages Of Empathy

We can say that empathy starts with intuition and ends with prediction, and prediction is when one person is able to foretell the emotional responses of the other. The stages of empathy are thus given as:

1. Intuition

2. Connection

3. Consideration

4. Prediction

5. Motivation

The first stage of intuition involves one person naturally intuitive towards the other as with intuition of the other person's emotions and feelings or thought processes; the next stage of empathy or a feeling of connection is created. The connection between two people naturally leads to a feeling of mutual consideration and the next stage of predicting each other's responses to situation. In some cases empathy could be mutual although in many cases as in a relationship between a therapist and her patient, the empathy could be one sided. After the connection is established and there is a deep sense of consideration for the others feelings, and an understanding as to why the person is feeling in a particular way, one person who empathizes with the other is able to move to the next stage of predicting the emotional responses. Understanding the response patterns in other people is an essential part of connecting and relating to them closely and would definitely suggest the ability of being in the shoes of the other. The last stage of empathy deals with the more directional aspect as in the case of teacher or therapist there is a need to motivate or influence the other person following an empathetic connection. In fact the empathy may have been established to influence the other person to attain some goals or reach some targets. So influencing and motivating the other person is an integral part of empathy and is a tacit goal of empathetic relations.

Apart from the five stages of empathy discussed, empathy could involve subsequent feelings of friendship, love, rapport, admiration, dependence and this would depend on whether the empathy is between a teacher and a student, a therapist and a patient, a leader and his followers or between lovers or friends. From a psychological point of view, empathy would involve fulfilling the safety and security needs of other individuals and also their love and a sense of belonging. Our need for Empathy are thus somewhere in between the love-attachment-belongingness (psychological) needs of individuals and the safety-security needs of individuals and the need for empathy exists in every individual and is manifested in both the forms of giving and receiving empathy.

Individuals fulfill their love and find a sense of belonging, needs created by relating to others and empathy uses love and belongingness to provide safety and security. Thus the purpose of empathy as explained with Maslow's hierarchy of needs theory is to make the other person happy by providing a sense of security and lending support as is the goal of empathy could mean a positive influence of one person on the other. Empathy highly enhances social interaction as it adds elements of familiarity, connectedness and consideration between people and help to instill and maintain human values.

WHY IS EMOTIONAL INTELLIGENCE IMPORTANT?

An emotionally intelligent individual is both highly conscious of his or her own emotional states, even negativity—frustration, sadness, or something more subtle—and able to identify and manage them. These people are also especially tuned in to the emotions others experience. It's easy to see how a sensitivity to emotional signals from within and from the social environment could make one a better friend, parent, leader, or romantic partner. Fortunately, these skills can be honed.

Many people are not completely aware how important emotional intelligence is in their lives. We attempt to read many books and articles about this matter just for the knowledge, but we ignore the fact that if we apply emotional intelligence in our daily life and work, it could lead us to somewhere else that we never expected.

The key skills of emotional intelligence could be learned by anyone, at any time. Imagine if you are able to overcome, control and get over your daily life stress with just being emotionally aware of everything that goes right there around you.

Emotional intelligence could be summarized in the ability to express your emotions and to control them at the same time, understand and interpret to others feelings.

There are four easy steps that can lead you to the emotional intelligence you always wished to have;

The first one is sensing the emotions: you should concentrate and accurately perceive the message someone tries to tell you, this actually involves not only understanding the person's intended words but also watching the non-verbal signs, body language and facial expressions.

The second one is reasoning with emotions: we should use our emotions to promote thinking. Emotions help in prioritizing what we pay attention and react to. This means that emotions play a very big part in guiding our minds to believing things that might or might not happen. We naturally react to things that attract our minds.

The third one is understanding emotions: emotions may carry whole different meanings at many times, some people can express their anger in an indirect way, this can actually be very obvious in the example of the angry boss; he can scream, shout and give you a very hard time just because he has an issue related to your work, or he experienced a bad morning with his wife. We should never get confused in understanding the reasons behind people's reactions and that's why training yourself to have emotional intelligence can help you in this matter.

The fourth and last one is managing emotions (the ability to manage your emotions): Emotions are valuable, and offer a bounty of benefits. Once we're able to process and cope with them effectively, we can then learn a lot about ourselves and our needs. If you feel something, let it out, do not engage yourself in another action hoping you can distract your feelings, this can lead you to many problems.

Managing and controlling your emotions and feelings are very important; it is a step towards reaching the emotional intelligence of knowing how to perfectly understand people around you with the least words and actions they make.

Despite the fact that emotional intelligence lacks the volume of quantitative empirical cognitive research that IQ has, the research in the field of cognitive learning has suggested that emotional intelligence is a key fundamental aspect of learning. According to a report published by the National Center for Clinical Infant Programs, the level of success that a student has learning new material boils down to their individual levels of confidence, self-control, curiosity, their ability to communicate, their cooperativeness, their elatedness and their intentionality. All these traits are aspects of emotional intelligence.

More recently social scientists are beginning to uncover the relationship of emotional intelligence to other organizational psychologies, such as leadership, group performance, individual performance, interpersonal exchange, performance evaluations, and change management. Humans are social beings and as such our level of success when dealing with people is intimately linked with our level of emotional intelligence.

Our Heart and Soul never call for negativity or reactivity, but a considered, emotionally mature response.

In our never-ending journey of unfolding our infinite potential, emotional maturity can be thought of as a next step in the evolution of our humanity and the opening of greater, conscious awareness to our self and to others.

So, some questions for self-reflection are:

Do you ever feel you need to change the way you respond to others?

How do you feel when others challenge or disagree with you?

Do you find yourself feeling fearful, angry or anxious? Do you know why?

How do you respond to others' feedback?

Are you ever taken back by the way you react to others?

Do you ever feel afraid about exploring your emotions? Why?

Do you consider yourself to be emotionally mature? What would others say?

IMPROVING YOUR LEVEL OF EMOTIONAL INTELLIGENCE

Researches and scientists see the intelligence quotient, also known as I.Q., as fixed, meaning that it does not change throughout one's lifetime. E.I. differs greatly from I.Q. in that E.I. can be improved through a combination of life experience, maturity, conscious thought and perseverance. You can improve your level of emotional intelligence by doing the following:

Reflect back to the most recent time you can remember of when you had hurt somebody's feelings when they got close to you and trusted you, study what your reactions were at the time and analyze what you said that inflicted emotional pain on the other person. Try to put yourself in shoes of the other person' and empathize with them, try to feel what they feel like you were in that position. In this drill, you will effectively increase your understanding of empathy thereby increasing your level of emotional intelligence as a result. Rather than you finding fault with others, work on developing a mindset of positive thoughts and try to come up with possible solutions on a given problem. Remember that everyone you deal with is human and as humans we make mistakes.

Also by being human we have the ability to learn from our mistakes and by creating a positive attitude we can effectively coach other people and ourselves to move forward instead of blaming other people or events for mistakes. Then you should now come to the realization that in order to succeed in this game we call life, it becomes important to have a high level of one to one communication with those the people around you. You are, for the most part, helpless without other people to help you along the way. By better understanding their emotional needs you will be able to communicate with them more effectively and more accurately thus paving the way to your own personal success.

What You Need To Be Emotionally Mature

1. The ability to deal constructively with reality

To deal with reality in a constructive manner, we must face truth, the facts, rather than deny them. Running from problems or hoping they do not exist does not make them go away. Regardless of how unpleasant they may be at times, facing the facts is the first step to dealing with any situation. When people have difficulty facing reality, they resort to all sorts of unhealthy ways to deal with the unpleasant feelings and pain. They try to soothe themselves with alcohol, drugs, or any other way that temporarily masks their reality and pain. There are healthy and constructive ways to cope that lead to greater emotional maturity and growth. It may not be the easiest path to take, but it leads to healing, lasting comfort and hope.

2. The capacity to adapt to change

Change is not always easy. It can turn our world upside down at times and cause a great deal of stress. Whether the change is minor, like having to change our plans for the day, or more significant, such as moving to a new home, changing jobs, getting married or divorced, adapting to change is to make necessary adjustments. Sometimes the most important adjustment is in our attitude. Change can annoy us as it disrupts our routine and expectations, but we can choose to accept it and allow ourselves time to get comfortable with change.

3. A relative freedom from symptoms that are produced by tensions and anxieties

The symptoms produced from tensions and anxieties can include physical distress (headaches, stomach problems, rapid heart rate) and emotional distress (worry, restlessness, panic). Anxiety is a major mental health problem affecting millions of people every day. It negatively affects all levels of people's lives--their mental and physical health, relationships, work. To live free of its destructive symptoms and consequences is to cope with life stress in a healthy manner, learn to relax, release worries, and develop inner peace.

4. The capacity to find more satisfaction in giving than receiving

People who give of themselves--their time, attention, help, finances, or what they are able-- are generally more fulfilled and happy than those who do not. People who are primarily takers are more likely to use others for their own personal gain and are often considered selfish, stingy, and/or greedy. Like the old scrooge, they end up miserable. Givers, on the other hand, want to contribute and make a positive difference in this world. It is healthy to give cheerfully and willingly as it contributes to our sense of purpose and helps us connect with others and our society.

5. The capacity to relate to other people in a consistent manner with mutual satisfaction and helpfulness

Like I always say, life is all about relationships. We relate to others every single day--whether it is a relative, co-worker, neighbor, or stranger, our lives are intertwined with others. Love and respect are two key factors to relating successfully to others. Unlike dysfunctional relationships, healthy relationships are stable and provide deep satisfaction and joy.

6. The capacity to sublimate, to direct one's instinctive hostile energy into creative and constructive outlets

If we were to release all our frustrations and anger on the world, we would have a hostile existence. Instead, we can take that energy and direct it into something good and productive. It has long been said that sports is a great outlet of extra energy. Anything that is positive, constructive and creative can redirect our energies and put them to good use. A basketball player once told me that the court is where all his angry energy was released. He redirected his hostile energy in an acceptable way within specific guidelines and limits. It gave him a constructive outlet and helped him to really enjoy what he was doing without hurting others and/or himself.

7. The capacity to love, Love is the greatest power in the world

There's hardly any exact definition for love, because its that inexplicable beautiful feeling As humans, we are born with the capacity to love. The greatest differences between us are how we communicate our love.

Self-love is not opposed to the love of other people. You cannot really love yourself and do yourself a favor without doing people a favor, and vise versa. ~Karl Menninger

Experience is not what happens to you, it's how you interpret what happens to you. ~Aldous Huxley

Maturity has more to do with what types of experiences you've had, and what you've learned from them, and less to do with how many birthdays you've celebrated. ~unknown

TYPES OF EMOTIONAL INTELLIGENCE

Emotional Intelligence consists of five basic components namely self-awareness, self-regulation, motivation, empathy and social skills. The first three competencies are intra-personal and concern your ability to know and manage yourself. Empathy and social skills are inter-personal competencies and concern your ability to interact and get along with others. The better your intra-personal skills, the easier it becomes to express your inter-personal skills. Mastering these skills will allow you to live a better, happier and more successful and fulfilled life.

Self-awareness is the first component of emotional intelligence. It is the ability to know which emotions you are feeling and why. When you understand your emotions, it is easier for you to acknowledge and control your emotions and prevent your feelings from ruling you. You also become more confident as you do not let your emotions get out of control. Being self-aware also enables you to take an honest look at yourself and better know your strengths and weaknesses, and work on these areas to achieve better outcomes for yourself and others.

Recognizing our own emotions and how they recognize our own thoughts and behavior is what is essential for proper performance in workplace. Knowing our strengths and weakness and developing self-confidence is the prime for success in career.

Self-Regulation is the ability to control your emotions and impulses and choose the emotions that you want to experience instead of being the victim of whatever emotions arise. In self regulation you are a complete master over your emotions and when you are able to manage your emotional state, it becomes easier for you to think before you act and this prevents you from making impulsive and careless decisions. This skill also allows you to transform negative exhausting emotions into more positive and productive ones. Regulating ourselves is an essential component of Emotional intelligence. It is important to manage change that life brings in and for this we require self-regulation. Changes are the one which never change and so regulating ourselves to adapt to the new and different environ is essential.

Motivation : The third component of emotional intelligence is motivation. This is about using your emotions to remain positive, optimistic and persistent rather than negative and pessimistic. When you have a high degree of emotional intelligence you tend to be very motivated, productive and efficient in everything they do. You also use your emotions positively to take the right actions to persist and achieve your goals even in the face of considerable adversity or difficulty. Motivation is the ability to remain optimistic and to keep ourselves going even in case of failures and setbacks is called as motivation. Motivation is that internal power that you find when there is no reason to move foward, its that feeling you have after you have failed that makes you want to keep trying even when it looks stupid. Motivation is the one which makes us move towards our goals and desire. Facing organizational commitments, learning to improve performance, setting up challenging goals and being ready to seize opportunities is the most essential in today's corporate environment. All these can be done only through motivation.

The combination of all these competencies together make up the Emotional Intelligence quotient and possessing these skills are very important to succeed in the highly competitive, fast-moving, hi-tech world.

The corporate industries we have in the world today demands something more than powerful IQ. It sustains and takes hold of any individual with various social and personal competencies that allow them to regulate and manage the emotions of themselves and others around them. This ability to regulate the emotions with respect to the environment is known as Emotional Intelligence

Empathy is the fourth component of emotional intelligence. It is the ability to truly recognize and understand the feelings and point of view of people around you. Empathetic people usually possess the ability to listen effectively and accurately to others and are usually very excellent at managing relationships, improving communication; building trust and relating with others. Empathetic people are people you want to open up to , they have a way of making you talk about deep things you never want to talk about ,they are good listeners and if you are empathetic then it means You're able to understand the needs, wants and feelings of your subordinates and their situational issues. Having empathy, you're more likely to know what motivates workers to be more productive and pleased with their jobs, its like you've studied them and can feel what goes on in their head. You also have more of a team mindset and you , which means you're more open to improving team relationships and environmental issues that affect health and productivity. You can also better recognize desired traits in job candidates.

The fifth component of emotional intelligence are social skills. People with Social skills are the life of a party, emotionally intelligent people have good social skills and are excellent at building and maintaining relationships. When you are highly emotionally intelligent, you no longer focus on your own success first and you always have other's best interests in mind, you are constantly trying to see what you can do for people, what you can contribute. You always promote an environment where people cooperate with each other instead of compete with one another and you always help others develop and grow.

BENEFIT OF EMOTIONAL INTELLIGENCE

Your emotional intelligence (EI) is the ability to control and use your emotions in a constructive and productive manner.Its about making the best use of emotions to your benefit and to the benefit of others. It is very important to leadership and for successful relationships and I would advice anyone planning on taking leadership responsibilities to get trained properly in the use of emotional intelligence. It's your ability to intuitively communicate so effectively that you inspire others while not being derailed by upsetting or extreme circumstances to respond most appropriately as opposed to react in haste. Most times leaders are usually hated by their subordinate because they fail to consider the feelings, they use their powers and authority as superiors to behave irrational towards their staffs and this is because they are not emotionally intelligent, emotional intelligent leaders are loved by the staff because they have a way of correcting their subordinates without ridiculing them. Leaders who are strong in this skill have good emotional self-control, think clearly even when they are experiencing strong emotions, and make decisions using both their heart and their head. This does not mean they don't have sensual feelings. On the other hand they are passionate people just like you and I. However, they understand that a man in passion can sometimes get in the way of their personality, making them tough as a nail and hard to relate to so they need temper their passion immediately.

Along with the general competencies for various job roles, you may want to focus on your company's key competencies and this is where emotional intelligence skills come in again. If your company focuses on great customer service, for example, you may want to focus on customer service-related competencies. Likewise, if your company's progress is centered on fast innovation, this would suggest a greater emphasis on creativity and innovation competencies. Leaders high in emotional intelligence are connected to the people around them. They present as authentic and empathetic, willing to practice expansive thinking, constantly seeking to include and understand rather than exclude and ignore. This means resilient and empowering leadership that isn't afraid of others opinions and doesn't feel the urge to have the final decision or always be proved correct. These leaders are centred and in control of both themselves and the world around them, which inspires confidence and trust, creating an atmosphere where employees energetically collaborate to produce the best possible results for the business.

The question is - who do we think of when we reflect on our own personal experiences of emotionally intelligent leadership? The sad truth is that, for most of us at least, there's a relative paucity of these people in the places we work. The majority of businesses still thinks of emotions and feelings as valueless and reward people not for HOW they get results but WHAT results they deliver. As a result, when we consider our own experiences, we are far more likely to recall distracted and busy leaders that don't have time to listen or who don't really listen even when they're sitting in front of us watching our mouths move.

The good news is emotionally intelligent leaders are not a fictional narrative , they are out there in organizations somewhere; and some companies are even investing and looking to foster and encourage leaders in their organizations. These businesses not exactly doing anything beyond the ordinary but they're simply accepting that there is a better way of doing things. They believe that creating a better place to work is achievable, and that assessing and developing the necessary skills is very much easy and achievable, it's has actually been a tried and tested practice that has been around for years.

These organizations are constantly looking to determine and instil the five components that all emotionally intelligent leaders should have in common; we have discussed these components in previous chapters. They are trying to build leaders who:

1. Understand and read the meaning behind thier own feelings

2. Can effectively express what they feel

3. Can 'Tap into' their feelings and into the emotions of others, especially their subordinates and leaders

4. Manage facts and feelings to yield great results

5. Positively influence their own and the feelings of others

In order to hold effective emotional intelligence you must first be self-aware, we have talked about this component earlier. In a culture focused on quantifiable deliverable, that is making it big with the number of sales, decreased production time, increased cost benefits, etc. Self-reflection isn't a priority. I say make it a priority before it costs you money, your job or valuable relationships.

Why is it important to have emotional intelligence? The first and simplest reason I can give you is that it builds confidence. Self-assurance grows with heightened self-awareness to a life driven by purpose and an ability to execute one's goals for a greater good. Confidence is essential for healthy relationships and communication unhampered by disruptive, self-destructive emotions. So if your behavior in certain situations is predictably ineffective and unfulfilling, improve your emotional intelligence the same way you build other skills, by learning and practicing.

Most of us call it gut feeling, but now psychologists are calling those feelings emotional intelligence or EI. Emotional intelligence is something like your IQ. Your IQ score doesn't tell you how much you know it simply tells you what your capacity to learn and comprehend is. Your EI is a tad trickier to measure and there is a great deal of disagreement on how it should be done. However, scientists can agree that in general, people who have a high EI, meaning they can identify their own emotions and the emotions of others, tend to have certain behaviors. Here's a quick list of some of those behaviors.

1. Adaptability

Developing emotional intelligence allows an individual to understand the emotions or motives of others and as a result they are more willing to adapt to a situation than a person who can only understand what they personally are feeling.

2. Managing emotions in others

As we have mood swings, excessive ego, and emotional breakdown and stress it is best that we keep everything simple. So that we don't flare up and hurt other people, managing emotions is not really about us despite the facts that we have a lot on our plate, its about understanding that the emotions in others is a key leadership trait which allows the person with high EI to influence others. Understanding needs and feelings lends itself to developing courses of action that will fulfill those needs and at the same time accomplish what the leader wants accomplished.

3. Emotional control

Persons who have a high EI understand their own emotions and can analyze them rationally. So when they are faced with frustration or fear or anger, they are less likely to react to them instinctively and are more likely to act in a controlled and informed manner. Emotional control can sometimes be developed with emotional maturity , well there are quite a number of younger individuals who have been able to master emotional control than many adults. Emotional control keeps you in check and discipline you , it takes so much intentional effort to achieve this feat.

4. Less Impulsive

High Emotional Inteligence means bad news for marketers who take opportunity of people's impulse to buy products. People with high EI don't react impulsively but rather look at their feelings and make rational decisions without the interference of overwhelming emotional pull.

5. Strong relationships

Maybe one of the greatest advantages of elevated emotional intelligence is the ability to enter into and sustain strong and fulfilling relationships. Being able to understand and appreciate the emotions of others and not being driven by a "me first" need can result in more satisfying and less conflictive interactions with the people around you.

6. More optimistic face it.

We live in a culture that sees the glass half empty more than we see it half full. High EI develops high self-esteem which in turn gives the person the confidence to see the brighter side even in difficult situations.

7. Better stress management

Precisely because they have more self-esteem, self-confidence and an optimistic viewpoint of life, people with developed EI can handle more stress and pressure than others. Being able to identify stress points not as threats but simply as challenges to be met, changes the nature of the stress to a manageable condition. There are obvious advantages to developing emotional intelligence but there are also arguments over how that can be done. Some say it is simply an innate skill that you are born with. Others say you can improve it through training programs like emotional intelligence workshops. Whatever the answer is, it's obvious that understanding ourselves and the emotions of others has a distinct advantage in communications, relationships and personal behavior.

EMOTIONAL INTELLIGENCE
FOR LEADERS

It is usually easier to identify those who have high EQ. These people are very self-aware and take the time to reflect on their actions and emotions. They recognize what triggers certain emotions and how to handle them even under dire circumstances. They also know when they may have reached a "boiling point" and need to back off from a situation temporarily, review what has happened, and devise a solution. It is like hitting the pause button on a remote control.

In addition, they understand that for one to develop emotionally there are times when they may face criticism from others and they need to see this as an opportunity for growth; in other words it is viewed as a learning lesson. They are also willing to provide feedback to others on their team, but they do it in a manner that is helpful not hurtful. These individuals are also sensitive to others' feelings, so they know when they may have overstepped and need to offer an apology. This does take courage because many would rather avoid a situation versus getting into a conflict with another team member. It is much trickier to figure out those who have low EQ. Some may have excellent technical skills and have been successful in their career so far but when a crisis occurs they fall apart. Others may exhibit chronic emotional distress which includes being negative all the time, inconsistent in their behavior, and/or holds grudges. Unfortunately there is no magic formula or pill for these people to change from low to high EQ.

So what is a leader supposed to do? The first step is to delicately converse with the low EQ person about what is being observed amongst the team members and to collaboratively devise solutions to rectify the situation. It is a good idea to have an objective third person present (human resources, coach, or senior executive) to steer the conversation in a positive manner but also to be a witness to the reactions of the employee. If it is agreed upon that the person needs some assistance, the leader should handle this as quickly as possible. If it gets delayed, the employee could be less trusting of the leader and more problems could occur. If the employee resists taking action, it is then up to the leader to suggest a few alternatives - layoff, reassigning to another department, or suggesting other courses of action outside the workplace i.e. classes or therapy.

EQ is hard to detect during the interview process so leaders should consider different means to identify a candidate's EQ. Reference checks only go so far because the references may be fearful of lawsuits or other means of retaliation. Assessments and testing are helpful but are time-consuming and expensive. Multiple interviews over a period of time are a smart move because the interviewers can see if the candidate demonstrates consistent behavior. Ideally a combination of all of these should ensure that the final candidate has a high EQ.

Leadership involves dealing with people. Some folks are extroverts and some are introverts. The extroverts feel comfortable around social functions and in dealing with groups almost all the time. On the other hand, introverts tend to be shy and to focus more on individual interactions. Yet, being an extrovert is not an indication of emotional intelligence. Introverts can also show emotional intelligence or what has become commonly called as EQ. What exactly is this EQ? It simply means the capacity, skill and ability to manage one's emotions in relation to other people. Have you ever heard of the quote "people won't care about what you know until they know you care"? That is very true. People care less for knowledge than for emotional connection. And if you are able to connect emotionally to more people, you become a more successful salesperson, businessman or a leader.

Adolf Hitler, Winston Churchill and Barack Obama managed to connect emotionally with people and that is why they became very popular in their respective countries. Connecting emotionally is just one side of the coin. The other side is leadership. Emotional intelligence and transformational leadership go together. One of the tenets of transformational leadership is motivation and idealism. When you appeal to the values of people and to what they hold dear, you can easily sway them to your cause and make you popular. When you are able to do that, you can then sell your transformational agenda to them.

This is not an easy path to take. If you fail in engaging people emotionally, you will be exposed as a fraud and you can easily lose your integrity and your ability to influence people. But if you manage to balance them, you will be able to become an effective leader.

How Emotional Intelligence Helps You Become A Flexible Leader

Emotionally intelligent (EQ) leaders are flexible in adapting their leadership style to those they choose to lead. You will influence and engage employees by being socially savvy regarding which leadership style would be the most appropriate with certain personalities and in specific situations.

The Blanchard and Hersey Model of Leadership

As a leadership model, the best known example was developed by Ken Blanchard, the management guru who later became famous for his One Minute Manager series, and Paul Hersey. They created a model of situational leadership in the late 1960s that allows one to analyze the needs of the situation, and then adopt the most appropriate leadership style. The model has two fundamental concepts; leadership style, and development level.

Leadership Styles:

Blanchard and Hersey characterized leadership style in terms of the amount of direction and support that the leader provides to his or her followers. They categorized all leadership styles into four behavior types, which they named S1 to S4:

S1: Directing Leaders define the roles and tasks of the follower, and supervise them closely. Decisions are made by the leader and announced, so communication is largely one-way.

S2: Coaching Leaders still define roles and tasks, but seeks ideas and suggestions from the follower. Decisions remain the prerogative of the leader, but communication is much more two-way.

S3: Supporting Leaders pass day-to-day decisions, such as task allocation and processes, to the follower. The leader facilitates and takes part in decisions, but control is with the follower.

S4: Delegating Leaders are still involved in decisions and problem-solving, but control is with the follower. The follower decides when and how the leader will be involved.

No one style is considered optimal or desired for all leaders to possess. Effective leaders need to be flexible, and must adapt themselves according to the situation. However, each leader tends to have a natural style, and in applying Situational Leadership he/she must know his/her intrinsic style.

Development Levels:

The right leadership style will depend on the person being led - the follower. Blanchard and Hersey extended their model to include the Development Level of the follower. They stated that the chosen style of the leader should be based on the competence and commitment of his/her followers. They categorized the possible development of followers into four levels, which they named D1 to D4:

D1: Low Competence, High Commitment - They generally lack the specific skills required for the job in hand, however, they are eager to learn and willing to take direction.

D2: Some Competence, Low Commitment - They may have some relevant skills, but will not be able to do the job without help. The task or the situation may be new to them.

D3: High Competence, Variable Commitment - They are experienced and capable, but may lack the confidence to go it alone, or the motivation to do it well or quickly.

D4: High Competence, High Commitment - They are experienced at the job, and comfortable with their own ability to do it well. They may even be more skilled than the leader.

Development Levels are also situational. You might be generally skilled, confident and motivated your job, but would still drop into Level D1 when faced with a task requiring skills you do not possess. For example, many managers are D4 when dealing with the day-to-day running of their department, but move to D1 or D2 when dealing with a sensitive employee issue.

Leadership Development Matching:

Blanchard and Hersey indicate that the leadership style (S1 - S4) of the leader must correspond to the development level (D1 - D4) of the follower. In addition, it is the leader who must adapt, not the follower. To get the most of situational leadership, a leader should be trained in how to operate effectively in various leadership styles, and how to determine the development level of others.

What are your ideas and experiences related to situational leadership? You and your company leaders might from working with an executive coach as part of an emotional intelligence-based leadership development program.

Emotional intelligence in work place

Intelligence is the psychological feature or functioning of a human being's mind and it is being measured by IQ (intelligence quotient). But IQ alone is not the only determinant of a person's ability to get used and adapt with the complex situations of life and his work place efficiency. Intelligence based on emotions can be a factor for determining the success of a person at a work place or outside the work environment. Possessing a good IQ can help decide if you get hired, and EQ gets you fired or promoted. These two skills are common traits you'll find in high flying achievers globally and a combination of both determines the professional success. There is a very close linkage between an individual's intrapersonal function and his interpersonal skills. Here are examples called the 3 R's Concept.

1. RECOGNIZE

2. REDIRECT

3. REFLECT

Recognizing one's own feelings and redirecting those feelings (intrapersonal capacity) and reflecting that redirection of feelings in one's behavior for better communication, effectiveness in interactions and exhibiting greater understanding of one's environment. While human beings are able to relate on a more rational and emotional levels, emotions are the center of our energy, they are the power house of our life. An employee's emotional reaction and their work performance the pendulum has now swung towards recognition that employee emotions are unavoidable and they influence their work behavior and outcomes. The notion that emotions influences work performances are not a strange discovery, what is new that we have found a way to linking emotions to efficiency in work performance and its valuable consequences in organizations.

Your organization is made of people, processes, and property. For a long time, "common wisdom" has been that returns come from investing in the latter two. Yet, in the last decades, new research has challenged that assumption and is increasingly proving that a company's people are the differentiating factor.

In fact, for most businesses, products and property yield little competitive advantage. You develop a new process, and in a week your competitor replicates it. You increase efficiency and lower product cost, and next month a better version is being produced more cheaply in another country. You invest in specialized equipment - and so does the guy down the street.

So where can today's businesses find competitive advantage? With a mobile workforce, globalization, and on-demand information, products and property are not enough. Exceptional organizations are investing in their relationships with customers, employees, and leaders - and over the next decades the people side will increasingly become the only meaningful competitive advantage. If emotional intelligence helps build customer and employee loyalty, helps people innovate and perform, helps leaders build value, then these competencies are essential for world-class performance.

Emotional intelligence affects employee performance in multiple avenues. The employee's own EQ, the interaction between the employee, and the emotional tone - or climate - all significantly affect the way employees feel about work, and the effectiveness of the work they do.

Emotionally Attractive Leaders Create Lovable Companies

If you pause to ponder about the best work you've ever delivered, you'll probably realize you didn't do it all for yourself; you did it for that adorable boss or some other endearing leader who has been your hero in all aspects.

Recall the number of times you may have reached home aglow with a feeling of elation, reliving a positive encounter with an upbeat and supportive boss, perhaps savouring a lighter moment with him or a witty remark about your performance. The bounce that you feel, and the eagerness to get back to office to offer your very best, the 'Thank God It's Monday' phenomenon and the Friday Blues; that's the "afterglow" that lingers and gives you renewed energy to be more productive, and to bring your finest talents to work.

Inspiration is at the core of efficiency and employees react and respond best to leaders who exude warmth, and authentically invest time and effort to connect with them.

In today's global market place most powerful way to influence--and lead--is to be lovable.

The leaders control the switch that can alter the intensity of engagement of the employees of their organization. A leader's jaunty disposition allegorically oxygenates the blood of followers - it's a transfusion into the arteries of corporate ecosystem.

Studies indicate that since World War II, the human brain has been changing on the emotional front. The amygdala, which coordinates emotions, has grown 0.5 of one percent-that is "physiologically remarkable."

Emotions are infectious and leaders are the "emotional thermostats" of the groups and organisations they lead. A fine example to consider this would be Military forces. How would an "overwhelmed", "nervous", "irritated", "indecisive" or "inconsistent" commander effect troop morale and vigour? How would he energise and inspire his team to weather all storms and lay down their lives at a single command?

"Indecision," is transmissible." It can become incapacitating and habit-forming in an organization, as people take their cues from the leader's state of mind. We want our leaders to be predictable because there is comfort and safety in consistency. Predictability engenders trust and an impulsive leader elicits anxiety and, in some cases, even fear, both of which negatively affect performance and productivity.

Bosses who are lovable, emotionally attractive and charismatic draw people like a magnet. Their ceaseless energy and eternal optimism, ignites their followers to stretch beyond boundaries and deliver superlative performance. They harbour passion for what they do, and this spills over into their business relationships. They blossom because they love people and people love them. There is an emotional bond between the leader and those led. It is seen that organisations with upbeat, enthusiastic, and cohesive executive team are likely to yield better business results. The study also showed that the longer a company was managed by disjointed executive team that didn't get along well, the poorer its image and market returns.

Among the most admired leaders across the world, the following names have stood out owing to their charisma, ability to build a powerful emotional connection with their followers, and communication that inspired and electrified their audiences.

Winston Churchill, Steve Jobs, Mahatma Gandhi, Nelson Mandela, Jack Welch, Abraham Lincoln, Margaret Thatcher, Ronald Reagan, John F Kenned, Bill Clinton, Napoleon Bonaparte

Those with a strong vision were most admired, but motivational, caring, innovative, persistent and ethical qualities were also held in high regard.

For example, John F. Kennedy personified emotionally attractive leadership even before the concept was popularized. Self-awareness, spirited intelligence, self-will, image discipline, empathy and savvy connection to communication, audiences and relationships made him an adorable public figure.

An inspiring speaker, he related to the masses and connected with them on relevant issues. Genuinely likable, when JFK spoke, audiences wanted to concur with him. His tone, poise and deportment communicated credibility and responsibility. He declared a new re-awakening for America and political Washington... people believed. When he was assassinated, a bit of everyone was extinguished.

For charismatic leadership like his, the right blend of emotional intelligence and magnetic charm causes spectacular upshots. It sets the tone, connection and rapport to energize teams to higher levels of synergy and superior achievement. Organizations that cultivate emotional intelligence at the leadership levels experience high levels of team engagement, support for a wide array of initiatives, and a focus on excellence.

The law of reciprocity states that people will reciprocate emotional experiences. Sometimes they reciprocate in a direct reflection (back at you) and other times they reciprocate in an indirect defection (at the next Customer, a coworker or family member).

Research shows that up to 30% of a company's financial results (as measured by key business performance indicators such as revenue growth, return on sales, efficiency and profitability) are determined by the climate of the organization.

Roughly 50-70% of how employees perceive their organization's climate is attributable to the actions and behaviours of their leader. A leader constructs the ecosystem that determines people's moods at the office and their mood, in turn, affects their productivity and level of engagement.. In an organisation people continuously spread their own moods and are impacted by others' moods. When they work in groups, they literally can catch each others' emotions like viruses, a phenomenon known as emotional contagion.

Because employees pay great attention to their leaders' emotions, leaders can strongly influence the mood, and thus attitudes and performance, of their teams through emotional contagion.

There is significant research showing how emotions influence memory, perception and cognition. These factors influence every aspect of an employee's performance - in fact - what is "performance" other than the combination of thought, feeling and behavior?

The varied moods set off a chain reaction: A cranky and ruthless boss creates a toxic organisation filled with negative dark horses who ignore opportunities; an inspirational, inclusive leader generates acolytes for whom any challenge is surmountable. The final link in the chain is performance: profit or loss.

Good moods fire up good performance. The most effective executives display moods and behaviors that are relevant to the prevailing situation, with a healthy blend of optimism. They not only understand and appreciate how other people are feeling - even if it is blue or overwhelmed; but they also exemplify what it looks like to move ahead with hope and humor." The golden trio here is - 'optimism', 'hope' and 'humor'.

But in today's leadership environment, the stress is ever-present. Therefore if you want to be successful over time while maintaining your equilibrium, you have to develop a new skill... emotional talent." Be emotionally attractive. Your emotional attractiveness is directly proportional to your 'likability factor' and translates into how well you consistently produce "positive emotional experiences" in the lives of others, including your staff, prospects and clients.

A word of caution here - In order to be perceived as upbeat and reliable, the leaders cannot be putting on a game face every day. People are very sensitive and can easily see through strained or fake cheerfulness and inconsistent decisions. Leaders cannot sustain their effectiveness if they cannot sustain themselves.

It is required that an executive ascertains, through reflective analysis, how his emotional leadership drives the moods and actions of the organization, and modifies his conduct correspondingly.

How to elevate your emotional attractiveness quotient:

1. Establish Consistent Friendliness - Friendliness is a communication event. It's important for your people to perceive you as friendly. Over time uniformity in behaviour counts far more than first impressions.

2. Relevance is the extent to which a person is able to connect his or her interests, wants, and needs to another's "sweet spot." Mutual interests establish a higher level of relevance. You can accomplish more by

developing interest in people than you will in trying to get others interested in you.

a. Identify your frequent contact circle

b. Connect with others' interests

c. Connect with others' wants and needs

3. Empathy is the ability to accurately perceive and comprehend another person's internal frame of reference. It is based upon deep listening and the ability to pick up on more than words.

a. Show an interest in how others feel

b. Experience others' feelings

c. Respond to others' feelings

4. Realness is capability to be genuine and true. It is impossible to have a high EAQ without being genuine, true, and authentic. People who are authentic inspire trust and make others feel good about themselves. They have a strong sense of who they and what they value.

With an ever-expanding marketplace and increasing competition, possessing a high EA factor can be the one thing that distinguishes your business organisation from many others in the race, and can spell the difference between success and failure. It is about enhancing relationships at workplace, which will lead to more effective communication, increased cooperation, satisfied employees, and delighted customers and, ultimately, drive success of your teams and organisations.

LEADERSHIP LIFESTYLE
TO EMULATE

Many organizations are aware of the value of emotional intelligence to a leader's success, but uncertain about how to apply it. To gain the full benefit of EI in a leadership role, companies needed to better understand how to best grow EI among leaders.

Correlating leadership styles with emotional intelligence strengths makes it easier for organizations to identify different emotional styles among their leaders/managers and as a result place them in roles calling for their strengths. Because emotional intelligence is a skill and it's very easy to learn, companies can provide training and support for leaders who need to modify their leadership style to be more effective.

Leadership styles are often determined by the leader's emotional strengths, often expressed in four or five distinct clusters of emotional strengths: Self-Perception, Self-Expression, Interpersonal, Decision Making and Stress Management.

These 5 clusters also reflect five different leadership styles and much is gained by naming them in more commonly used terms i.e.: The Star, The Coach, The Social Worker, The Engineer, and The Physician makes it easier for everyone to comprehend the differences. The necessary skills among the 5 clusters are the same but the names have changed. A "Star" styled leader, for instance, is likely to call upon his/her self-awareness and self-confidence to lead while a "Physician" style leader is likely to leverage their ability to manage stress and "role with the punches" to manage. A "Coach" styled leader is often engaged in making certain their direct reports understand the rules and strategize for victory, while a "Social Worker" styled leader is always focused on others and attempting to achieve goals through other by better understanding them. Finally, the "Engineer" is all about tasks and problem solving and creating realistic objectives.

Of course, each of these leadership styles is shaped by their understanding and natural abilities but determining the style most needed for the task and finding a leader with the necessary style, has just become a lot easier. Now organizations can ask and scientifically identify the leadership style that matches the needs of the job. For example, what kind of task would likely require a "Star" type leader?

Tasks that require "Star" type leaders are those jobs what have ambitious objectives, requiring a positive attitude and ability to motivate others would be a simple description. What type of leader could best head-up a large public project, for instance? The "Social Worker" leader might be good fit here since he/she is likely highly skilled at connecting with people and sensitive to the needs of others.

This subject really requires much more space and time than we can give it here, but I am betting that you are beginning to get the picture. The picture of how results can be improved by matching Emotional Leadership Styles with the needs of the job and how many profits can be advanced by doing so.

In organizations the skills needed for SELF can be grouped into self-awareness (emotional awareness, accurate self-assessment, self-confidence) and SELF MANAGEMENT (self-control, transparency, adaptability, achievement, initiative, optimism). Other social awareness skill are social awareness (empathy, organizational awareness) and RELATIONSHIP MANAGEMENT (inspiration, influence, developing others, change catalyst, conflict management, teamwork and collaboration).

In the course of this book we have discussed and talked about self-management, self-awareness and empathy, it would be reasonable that this time we can talk about work place relationship in terms of relationship as a social awareness skill.

Relationship Management

The management of relationship has been a facet of business for as long as business transactions have existed. On the most basic level, Relationship

Management is about interaction with customers. From a broader perspective one can consider employees, suppliers and consumers as customers, the employees being the internal customers of the organization. Relationship Management deals with the treatment and management of partnerships, connections, linkages and chains between business entities.

For the purposes of this paper, we view Relationship Management (RM) as a conscious and planned activity. It would be misleading to suggest that there have not been relationships in business or any focus on relationships by companies. However, the thrust of RM, as expounded in recent times, points to a more tactical and strategic approach to focusing on the customer rather than a relentless focus on the competition.

After the economic downturn of the 90s, many companies started to examine the possible benefits to be gained from less negotiation strong-arming, closeness to suppliers and the establishment of constructive relationships with strategic stakeholders. This does not suggest that RM was founded in the US, or has not existed before then; the Japanese had perfected RM and value-concretization into an art form on the basis of social structure and communal creed.

RM itself has not just many types but many levels. The manufacturer has his suppliers and the end users as his customers; the retailer has the manufacturers and the end users as his customers, and manufacturer, the supplier and every organization with a tactical or strategic agenda have internal customers.

Different types of RM have been identified, ranging from the transactional, the collaborative and the formation of alliances, which is also known as partnerships or value-added exchanges. The alliance is a partnership with suppliers that involves a mutual beneficiary arrangement where cost-cutting ventures are jointly addressed by both buyer and seller, the seller being considered an extension of the buyer's organization. The business relationship between Japanese suppliers using JIT is a good example. For example Toyota holds a strong alliance even with its 3rd tier vendors. The result of such partnerships means added value, reduced production and transport costs, a more seamless supply and delivery network, and maintenance of exceptional quality, as per TQM considerations.

Traditionally, companies were preoccupied with rigorous competition, firm-induced and firm-controlled business strategies, focus on short-term profits and strategies and independent decision-making. This transactional existence meant a focus more on the competition than the customer, a concentration on short-term profits rather than long-term strategic gains and likelihood to be blind to opportunities for expansion and change. Today's strategically-minded companies are pre-occupied with partnership with other firms, collaboration and coaction, boundarylessness, joint decision-making and a focus on long term benefits. With today's business climate, one can easily foresee a rapidly changing business environment where manufacturers will have the most fruitful partnerships with every member of the supply chain and the consumers, a scenario where the manufacturer will run a 'virtual factory' with the effective and efficient use of value chain networks unlimited by geographical location or consideration.

RM functions on a strategic, a tactical and an operational level. Businesses that are product-oriented ensure effective performance of their products, in the design, the features and output; the production-oriented business (not to be confused with the product-oriented) believe in mass production at a cheap scale on the notion that the customer uses low-price as a singular consideration; sales-oriented businesses put a lot of stock in advertising, promotions and public relations while the customer-centric enterprise strives to understand its customers preferences and purchasing behavior and models its business activities to suit this. This is considered strategic RM. The operational level deals with automating the customer management process using computer applications and devices across market, sales force and service categories. Tactical RM deals with using the data from customer management computer applications to add value both to the customer and the company.

While it would be immensely useful to run a customer database to keep the organization in sync with full information with its customers, RM especially from a strategic perspective delves deeper than mere software; it deals with a 'pull' strategy, letting the wants and needs of the customer dictate what products and services are offered, rather than the other way round, using a production-oriented strategy to 'push' products and services that the consumers may or may not need, but which does not ultimately satisfy the customer.

Companies generate more revenue when they satisfy - and because of this retain- their customers. It is hereby propounded that the simple economic fact that customer retention is cheaper than customer attraction provides the customer with an intrinsic importance to business performance than anything else.

Relationship management: The final area you need to develop in raising your EQ is that of relationship management. We can look upon this trait in connection with your profession. This is the aspect of your EQ that enables you to succeed in inspiring other people and helping them to reach their full potential. It is also vital in negotiating successfully, resolving conflicts and working with others toward a shared goal. Your success in this final area is directly correlated to your success in the other three areas because management is all about successfully interacting with other people. At the end of the day isn't efficient management all about getting the work done?

LOW EMOTIONAL CAPABILITIES CAN RUIN YOU

Some time ago I observed at the place where I work that employees having low emotional competencies tend to lose their jobs even after being selected from hundreds of applicants who were interviewed. There was this employee joined the organization, during the faculty development programme was called to share her experiences but she refused by saying that she is not prepared, our director took her refusal as her shyness, nervousness to come in front and gave so much motivating examples from his own life and with expressing his disappointment due to her refusal and then again asked her to speak but all in vain because she took that behavior as insult failing to recognize her emotions and emotional responses and those of director's and reacted as a slave of emotions. She could not bear that incidence and never came back.

Emotional intelligence can help explain why employees with strong academic backgrounds or cognitive skills are not always the best team members and leaders. Emotional Intelligence shapes human behavior in diverse realms including workplace, community and schools. On the individual plane, it is found to relate to work performance, our ability to communicate effectively, build meaningful interpersonal relationships, resolve everyday problems, scholastic achievement, and even our potential to make moral decisions. Admitting the possibility of EI to amplify our understanding of how individuals behave and adjust to their social environment, it forms an area of immediate attention to HR managers and practitioners.

Bad emotional experience always takes its toll in terms of thwarted problem-solving ability, innovation, commitment, creativity and productivity. Diversity in appearance, food habits, beliefs, thought patterns, reactions, choices and so on define any and every workplace. Nothing could be easier to handle this except by honoring it. HR people need to ensure that staffers have means to express their varied beliefs and opinions. To encourage and stimulate healthy emotional climate among employees, HR managers should:

1) Promote open communication and honest feedback.

2) Emphasize that speaking about emotion within organization is fine.

3) Specify that loud thinking among team members is okay.

4) Enlighten staffers that it is no sin to admit some of management's ideas may be flawed.

5) Organize standardized training on Emotional Intelligence and competency building.

6) Stress the value of striking emotional bonds with one's allotted task.

7) Highlight the benefits of maintaining informal, cheerful and positive work spaces.

Emotional intelligence is supposed to factor as a crucial recruitment criterion along with other relevant technical skills or business knowledge. It should be considered or should be used for the recruitments of fresh staffs into organsations. In case of promotions and succession planning, EI should figure as a decisive factor, mainly if leadership roles are foreseen. Even while selecting and grooming people with good potential EI should be emphasized. Similarly training and development programs must spotlight EI. Through some emotional release session or team-building exercises, the fact is, today, more and more CEO's are passing on the mantle of responsibility as counselors to their workforce. The biggest imperative before all the leaders and business owners is to make sure that negative emotions do not end up creating negative spaces and negative consequences within organizations. Unleashing a culture of positivity and openness holds the key to effective emotion management in any company.

EI FOR THE SALESMAN

EQ enables you to maximize your own sales potential by firstly understanding yourself and then understanding how other people are made up - enabling you to communicate in a way that they would like, rather than from your point of view.

Emotional Intelligence is known as EQ which for the dyslexic people out there (of which I am one) does cause some confusion but highlights the recognition that EQ and IQ are similar; one is a measure of intelligence and the other a measure of the emotions.

Emotional Intelligence is more important than IQ.

Research shows that EQ in a commercial environment may actually be significantly more important than information processing abilities and technical expertise combined. In fact, some studies indicate that EQ is more than twice as important as standard IQ abilities. Furthermore, evidence increasingly shows that the higher one goes in an organization, the more important EQ can be. For those in leadership positions, Emotional Intelligence skills are believed to account for close to 90 percent of what distinguishes outstanding leaders from those judged as average. IQ gets you hired, but EQ gets you promoted.

So what makes a great sales person and can EQ help?

I am sure you have heard many times people referring to someone as 'a natural'. Or that someone can 'sell fridges to Eskimos'. These sales people have great people skills or EQ; they are in tune with peoples' emotions, body language and can read people. It's a gift. Like playing great golf.

I can remember when I was working in presales on an account. When we finished the presentation the sales guy said to me:

"That went well, don't you think?"

Went well!?! It was terrible, people were looking at their watches, there were no questions, and we really had not understood the client's issues as we spent most of the time telling them how great we were. I could not understand how he could have come away from the same presentation with such a different point of view. We were clearly in trouble, and needed to do some serious rethinking if we were going to win the account.

The difference between the sales guy and me was in gauging how the pitch went. He had not tuned in to the unspoken signals that the people in the room were giving out.

Almost everyone at a pitch will be polite and tell you the meeting was a positive one, and that they can see good things ahead, but is this verbal reassurance backed up by the other signals they give out? If you can't pick up on these signals - you won't win many accounts, and sales will be a short career.

Emotional Intelligence Decreases Workplace Stress

Social Responsibility

At work, as in relationships, you have certain choices you can make. You can act like a mature, thoughtful, empathic, and responsible person or you can indulge what Freud called in his personality theory the id. This nasty little piece of who we are was described by Freud as blind, instinctual, irrational strivings. If you give in to your id responses, you will show very little social responsibility and you will become an aggravating and difficult colleague. Being prepared to give and take, to understand the other person's point of view, to maintain perspective and keep a larger view, and be generous in your relationships with others will increase harmony and decrease workplace stress for you and your colleagues.

Interpersonal Relationships

It's not unrealistic to say that there two types of people in this world - the givers and the takers. When I'm involved in marriage counseling I do a quick assessment to see which end of the spectrum is the chief personal style of each partner. Obviously, if you have two takers and no compromise you will have a marital battleground where each partner slugs away to get as much they can from the other. If you have a giver and taker then you will find one person whose life opportunities are sacrificed to the selfish interests of the other. When you have two givers, you'll probably have a comfortable, generous, caring, reciprocal sharing relationship - you know you are on a winner. In many ways, you can see the same system operating in the workplace with some people fighting tooth and nail to win at every opportunity. Developing collaborative teams requires people to be sensitive and committed to building positive, respectful, sharing relationships. When these relationships are the dominant interpersonal characteristics of work teams everyone's workplace stress is reduced.

Stress Tolerance

Everyone has a different capacity to deal with stress and anxiety. Some people have, as they say, a short fuse and are unable to tolerate even the smallest amount of stress. This is a pain and misery to everyone around them who has to put up with their limited capacity to manage stress. We can improve our capacity to deal proactively and effectively with stress; we can increase our stress tolerance mechanisms. This requires us to be mature and thoughtful and not indulge ourselves in juvenile expressions of frustration and impatience.

Impulse Control

One of my research areas is ADHD and a key characteristic of some people with ADHD is a diminished capacity for impulse control and self-regulatory management. Unfortunately, there are too many people in the workplace who show a reckless disregard for even a small amount of impulse control. They seem to believe that they have an incontestable right to vent their emotional eruptions whenever they feel like it and without regard to others. The converse of this is the responsible person who doesn't elevate other people's stress levels but carefully and effectively deals with the pressures and stress that they are experiencing.

This is probably a little too technical and I certainly have glossed over some of the complexities of each of these personal styles but these are complex matters. I could have given a simple tip checklist to reduce workplace stress based on emotional intelligence but this wouldn't be fair to either the interested reader of this fascinating area of personality and cognitive theory. My message is fairly simple - if you want to manage personal stress and reduce workplace stress you have a responsibility to behave in a mature, emotionally intelligent way. Of course I know the response most people would make - I'm not the problem, it's my colleague who has very low emotional intelligence and creates all the stress in this organization. Well, let's begin as they say - physician heals thyself. Then, after ensuring that you are OK, work to develop behaviors that reflect emotionally intelligent groups. I agree with the Harvard research that highly skilled work teams do reflect high group emotional intelligence and are much more productive. I'm also certain that people lucky enough be working in groups with high emotional intelligence and strong interpersonal responsibility have much lower personal stress levels and cope much more effectively with workplace stress.

Some real life examples of the benefit of developing emotional intelligence in the workplace include:

1. Greater sales

A study of over 40 Fortune 500 companies revealed that sales people with high emotional intelligence out performed those with medium to low EI by 50%.

2. Greater productivity

That same study revealed that technical programmers who were measured in the top 10% of the emotional intelligence competencies were cranking out new software three times faster than those with lower measurements. Even more astounding, a Dallas based company who underwent measuring its entire staff determined that employees with a high EI were 20 times more productive than those with a lower score.

3. Stability of staff

Another Fortune 500 had been using personality assessment for years in an attempt to slow down turn over in its high turnover sales force with little success. By implementing EI assessments, and including EI topics like stress management, self-awareness and social skills, they were able to stop the brain drain and increase retention by 67%. The firm calculated it saved over $30 million by reducing recruiting and training costs and increasing sales through retention.

4. Worker satisfaction

A Midwest community bank was forced to cut staff by 30% due to the tough economic times we have experienced recently. The remaining staff was evaluated for their emotional intelligence which resulted in certain changes in organizational structure. People were assigned positions where there EI was best suited for the task. The result is the bank now produces more with fewer people because the fewer people are now better suited for their positions and find them more fulfilling.

5. Improved risk management

Two studies, one for retail operations and one involving the construction industry determined that there was a correlation between low emotional intelligence and theft or shrinkage. In addition, persons with a low emotional intelligence score were more likely to have accidents on the job.

6. Amazing customer service

A luxury car dealership whose entizre marketing plan was built on customer experience and customer service was expanding and wanted to make sure they hired the best customer oriented employees to staff the new facility. The dealership utilized an EI assessment test and EI interviewing techniques that were designed to uncover a high level of empathy in candidates. This process was used to select everyone from the GM down to the valet. One year after opening, the new dealership was rated in the top 10% of the auto companies 200 plus dealers for both sales and customer satisfaction.

7. Better organizational communication

A Towers Watson study of both U.S. and Canadian firms disclosed that companies who do a better job of communicating with their employees outperform those who do not financially. On average a company with an exceptional communications program delivered a 47% greater return to shareholders than the least communicative firms.

Could your organization benefit from assessing your staff's emotional intelligence? Can you see how including EI in training and personal development programs can help the bottom line? As a professional, you owe it to yourself to at least investigate the possibilities.

8. When a team is created it will create an environment of social interdependence and that can be a good thing or bad depending on how it is managed. If the team leader explains that the group will focus on team goals and requires the input of all team members to be successful, the result is a greater effort to collaborate. However if the team is set up as competitors ie "the first one to sell 100 widgets gets a big bonus' then you have a team that consists of individuals with individual goals.

9. EI and team work

Positive and effective relationships between team members have been demonstrated to be the superior emotional setting to drive results. Members who share a bond both professionally and personally will work harder to achieve success for those for the group than a team where those relationships have not been developed. Developing emotional intelligence through exercises and training can greatly improve the odds of effective team performance.

If you are a team manager you really set the tone. If you want the most out of your team, work to set an environment that develops the relationships not tears them down through competition

12 ELEMENTS OF EMOTIONAL INTELLIGENCE

Intellect can be measured by standardized IQ tests but there is no actual measure of the "EQ," or Emotional Quotient. Even without a test, it's obvious when someone has a high IQ and it's just as obvious when someone has a high EQ. Rather than try to measure it, though, it's more useful to look at the various elements that go into emotional intelligence.

While the IQ remains stable over a person's lifetime, the EQ can be developed. Acquiring and practicing the following elements will enable you to boost your EQ.

The first element of emotional intelligence is empathy. The ability to understand what other people are feeling will make you more sensitive and aware and will result in more meaningful relationships.

The second element is the recognition that your actions have consequences. This understanding will enable you to make conscious choices in your life and to avoid unnecessary difficulties.

Third on the list is good judgment. The gift of making well-thought-out decisions and seeing people for who they really are will maximize the possibilities of success in all areas of your life.

Number four is personal responsibility. When you hold yourself accountable and don't blame anyone else for your mistakes or misfortunes, you are empowered to change things for the better. Other people respect you, because you own up to your part in your relationships.

The fifth element is insight. The ability to see yourself clearly and to understand your own motivations allows for the possibility of personal growth. Insight into others allows you to have a greater impact in your relationships.

Element number six is mental flexibility. Being able to change your mind or to see things from different points of view makes it possible for you to navigate all sorts of relationships and to succeed where other, more rigid thinkers would fail.

The seventh element is compassion. Being honest with yourself can be painful but with a kind and gentle attitude, it's much easier. This type of compassion facilitates personal transformation, while compassion toward others supports deeper, more loving connections.

The eighth element is integrity. Following through on commitments and keeping your promises creates much good-will in personal and professional relationships and promotes success in both arenas.

Ninth on the list is impulse control. Thinking before speaking or acting gives you a chance to make deliberate, even sophisticated choices about how you present yourself to others. Not acting out of primitive impulses, urges or emotions avoids social embarrassment.

The tenth element is the ability to defer gratification. It's one thing to want something but the ability to put off having it is empowering. Mastery of your needs allows you to to prioritize around life goals.

Number eleven on the list is perseverance. Sticking with something, especially when it's challenging, allows you to see it through to completion and demonstrates to others that you are dependable and potentially a high achiever.

The twelfth and final element is courage. Emotional courage (as opposed to the physical variety) is the ability to do the right thing, see the truth, open your heart and trust yourself and others enough to be vulnerable, even if all this is frightening. This causes others to hold you in high regard.

All these elements combine within you to make up your emotional intelligence. With a high EQ, even a simple person is at an advantage in life. Without it, even someone with the most brilliant intellect is at a disadvantage.

EMOTIONAL INTELLIGENCE IN THE HOME: RAISING EMOTIONALLY INTELLIGENT CHILDREN

Parents need to be emotionally intelligent to have any influence on teens which will allow them to become socially conscious while remaining stable and flexible in their emotions.

When a parent interacts with a child, especially a teenager, certain stress levels are brought in. The parent needs to keep this stress under control as this can be easily perceived by the teenager. This stress could lead to the child finding interaction constantly irksome and could cause the child to avoid the situation where he has to talk to people, basically this is why certain kids are extremely shy and avoid social life. Accept the fact that as a parent you are also a human and have your own needs of time and space. Let the teenager know this firmly enough and it is almost sure that the teen will accept the fact and live with it. Be consistent in all your dealings with their problems and even if they find your decisions irksome, they will still respect it for the constancy that you show.

Let not any feeling of guilt come into any dealings with your teenager. Children are always quick to spot such feelings and more than likely to take advantage of it. If you are feeling guilty in any way, better to correct the situation that has caused this guilt. Show your children the respect that his fledgling and developing personality has come to expect. Listen to their problems and the suggestions that they have and never lay down the law. Explain your situation in an adult manner. Teenagers will respond when you put the onus of understanding on them.

Emotional resilience learned early in life assists in recovering from misfortunes and disappointments, thus fostering emotional health. Teaching your child to be emotionally resilient will help him/her be in control and build confidence to work through challenging situations effectively. Becoming emotionally resilient in childhood will provide a basic foundation for your child's emotional health in adolescence and adulthood.

Emotions shape your child's interactions with others and affect his or her behaviors resulting from those interactions. In order to avoid conflict, or address situations adequately when it arises, your child should learn to understand his or her feelings, be able to identify them, and regulate them. It is important to teach children there is a whole gamut of emotions that can be expressed in various ways. However, knowing how to express them in a meaningful way will help your child in solving social conflicts and maintaining relationships. One way of promoting development of emotional competence is to help your child develop vocabulary that expresses feelings. Parents can also assist their children in recognizing various emotions and teaching them that emotions can be changed by their thinking.

Emotions are driven by behaviors. However, children must learn that emotions should not take control over their actions. It is crucial for children to know that expressing feelings helps in preventing and resolving problems. They need to be taught that bottled-up feelings lead to misunderstandings, anxiety, anger, and depression.

When your child does not express emotions, he or she is more likely to experience angry outbursts that might come from being sad, embarrassed, or frustrated. Perhaps, your child feels guilty about something he or she did, is afraid, or feels helpless and chooses to express those negative feelings of emotional stress with angry outbursts. This inability to deal with stress in a constructive way most of the time stems from the lack of understanding one's own emotions, emotions of others, and lacking the ability to express feelings effectively.

Signs of Emotional Fragility

- ☐ Regression of behaviors
- ☐ Withdrawal
- ☐ Excessive clinginess
- ☐ Bedwetting
- ☐ Nightmares
- ☐ Aggression

One of the most important things a parent can do to foster a child's healthy emotional development is to promote positive family communication. That includes positive reinforcement, which is praising your child for positive behaviors, giving encouragement, and avoidance of negative criticism when expected outcomes are not achieved. Also, providing consistency is extremely important for a child's emotional health, as it aids in avoiding ambiguity and uncertainty. If a child knows what's expected of him or her, they will most likely comply, thus avoiding frustration, anger, and possibly humiliation.

Younger children might be more open and willing to express their feelings. In adolescence, family communication might become more challenging as the teen tries to suppress their feelings in an attempt to resolve them alone. Parenting teenagers requires patience and the ability to be supportive. Frequently, conversation with your teen at home might be extremely difficult. However, your teen may try to open up while riding with you in a car where there is no eye contact, thus the confrontation seems to be less intimidating. Building a sound foundation of emotional resilience in childhood will help your adolescent achieve emotional health. Should getting through to your child become impossible, or he or she become withdrawn and exhibits signs of emotional instability, don't be afraid to seek help.

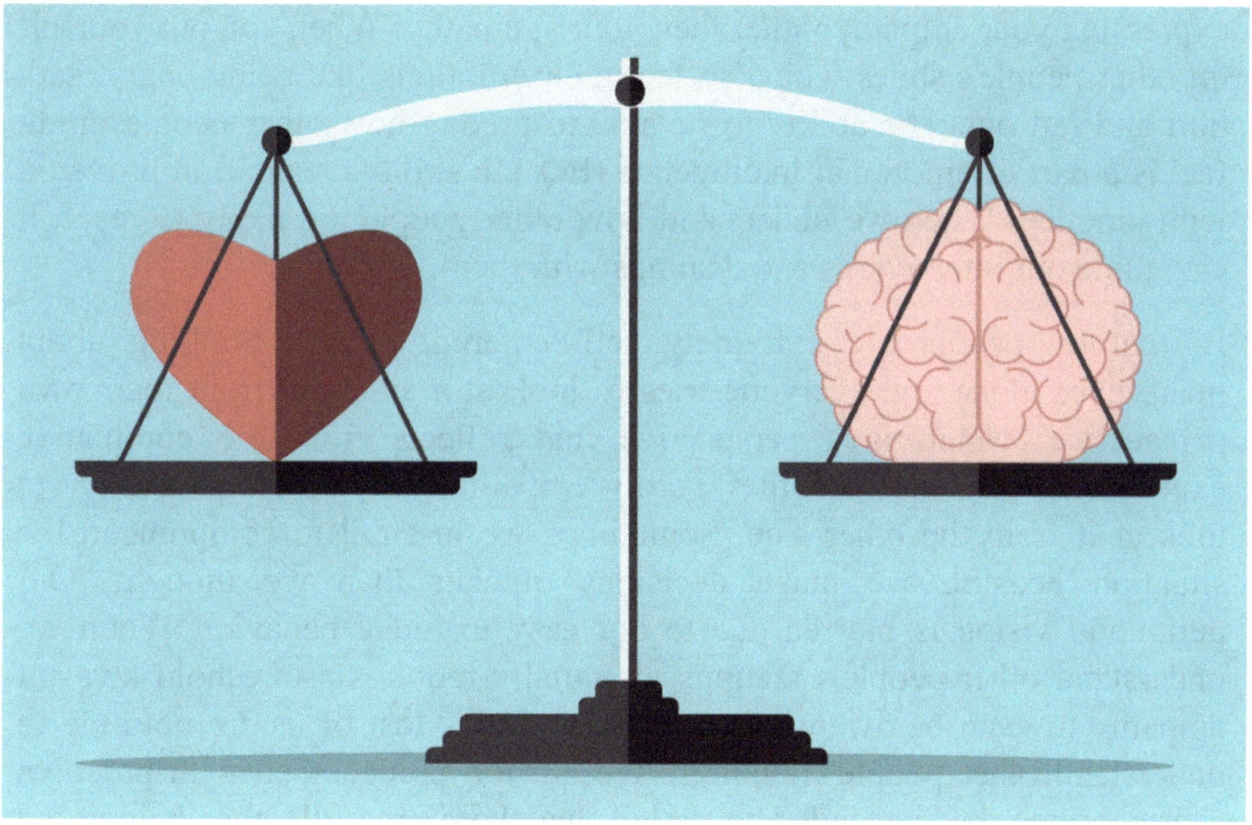

UNDERSTANDING THE EMOTIONS OF OTHERS

As hard as you may try to understand other people's situation and suffering, you'll not find it easy to relate with unless you go through the same circumstance. You will find it hard to understand their needs but if you are sensitive enough to feel what they feel, I am sure there is no problem expressing your empathy rather than your sympathy. When you put yourself on other people's shoes, you also feel their emotions like being angry, sad, hurt and left out. The ability to be able to predict how other people might feel is a part of emotional intelligence (EQ), a skill we can all improve on with practice. When we understand how other people are likely to react, it can guide our interactions and dealings with them.

By nature, people are extremely self-centered, always thinking about themselves alone and everyone tries to look at a situation from their own perspective, which is a perspective that reflects from the cumulative experiences of their lives, they hardly empathize any situation and try to look at it from the other side. Sometimes we just fail to comprehend the situation because we make decisions quicker than we thought. Our peripheral vision is blurred due to our easy to judge behavior. When we understand other people's feelings, it actually requires a threshold level of empathy to even be aware of what others feel. Most of us are not able to understand other people's feelings. We are too preoccupied with our own shortcomings that we failed to notice that there are still other beings out there who suffered more than we've been through. Though life is a matter of choice; our willingness to listen and understand others predicament can help boosts their morale. This is easier said than done. In reality, we are quick to make assumptions without digging deeper what makes them act or do such foolish actions that made them suffer than satisfied. I can understand that it is really difficult to feel what other people feel because some people are not willing to listen. We just need to regard people not on what they do but what their situation is because when it comes to understanding others, we seldom use our heart. Most often than not, we use our mouth to speak harsh words to others rather than let our emotions speak the truth.

We are more thoughtful when we listen with our hearts than our ears. We need to learn how to accept our mistakes before we can understand the mistakes of others. Most sensible people understand what they do. But it does not mean that they are mean. It just happened that they focused mostly on themselves rather than on other people you will find out that people who frequently have outbursts of anger, depression or flamboyant enthusiasm are generally disapproved of in the early stage of their childhood. There are some children who suffered emotional trauma in their formative years because of parents' neglect. True, we have to be patient in understanding their situation but it doesn't mean that we are going to tolerate such display of inappropriate behavior. If they are not corrected right now, then they will become liabilities of the society than assets.

But never ever assume everything is fine just because someone isn't having a nervous breakdown. We all have our individual problems, angst and upsets in life. We just have to be sensitive with the underlying currents that made them who they are. It gives us an advantage in trying to help. Emphatic understanding is very important especially if we want to know what others have been through.

Although many people have heard of empathy, (psychics who are able to sense or feel the emotions of others), few people fully understand what it means to possess empathic psychic abilities. People naively assume that this ability is a great and wonderful gift, and that it does not come at a cost to the psychic who possesses it. The truth is, this rare talent can also be a deadly burden to bear.

These psychics come with wide ranges of sensitivity. On one end of the spectrum are the emphatic psychics who can only vaguely recognize other people's feelings, while on the other end there are the powerful psychics who feel people's emotions as though they were their own. People who are able to relate with people on an emotional or empathetic level is called an empath, To be a compassionate person, we have to accept the kind of person we are and embrace our good values. The very essence of being compassionate is the eagerness to show empathy, to feel and help others with their suffering. This feeling helps us to generate more positive thoughts, real emotions and acts as a starting point for developing happiness within ourselves. Admittedly, it can be wonderful to be able to understand another person's feelings, and to be able to understand them and to help them cope with their feelings if they need help; empathic psychics are often skilled at emotional healing therapy. This is a process in which the psychic can share the burden of an extreme emotion, thereby lessening the pain that it is causing the patient. Alternatively, a psychic can guide a patient through difficult emotional distress by using their sensitive, intimate understanding of a patient's emotional state of mind.

How Can We Develop A Kind And Compassionate Mind

To develop a kind and compassionate mind it's going to take a lot of practice, but you will find a way to handle it. You can start by feeling compassionate for yourself every day. It might sound uncomfortable to imagine this. But try and say to yourself loudly so you can hear yourself say at any time of your day, make positive words of declaration every day say to yourself "I am a kind and compassionate person". Make it a priority to stay in conducive environment that is quiet, where you are relaxed, pause, slow down and spend at least three minutes every day to take deep breaths and get your head space. Reflect on all the wonderful qualities you would like to have as a person who is kind, loving, compassionate and someone who is full of life. Now, understand each emotion and find an opportunity to express that emotion. Imagine the kind person you are, feel it and do something as an act of kindness. Imagine the loving and compassionate person you are and feel it. See how your thoughts change, how your body reacts, what sensations you feel, how you see the world around you right when you feel these emotions. Take each quality and imagine being a person who thinks feels and act with this quality.

EMOTIONAL INTELLIGENCE AND SELF-ESTEEM

Emotional intelligence (EQ) is about being aware of your emotions. If you have a high emotional intelligence you know what you are feeling from moment to moment, and in most cases you also know why you are feeling as you do. Furthermore, you know what it is that you need to do in order to change your emotions in situations when you wish to feel differently. Emotional intelligence thus makes you more aware of your personal needs and it increases your ability to take good care of yourself. Having a high emotional intelligence cannot be unaccompanied by high self-awareness. Thus, if you have a high EQ you also know yourself well. It is easier to build a high self-esteem (i.e. to develop a good relationship with yourself) when you know yourself. How can you accept and love someone you don't know? For this reason, self-esteem and emotional intelligence go hand in hand. As you raise your emotional intelligence you also learn to understand yourself better, accept yourself (including both negative and positive emotions), satisfy your personal needs and value yourself more. Everything gets easier when you improve the relationship with yourself.

Emotional intelligence is not only about understanding oneself, but also about understanding other people. With a high EQ you can enter a room full of people and immediately get a sense of how the people in that room are feeling at that moment. You can understand other people's needs better, and this makes it easier for you to help them to satisfy those needs. This makes it easier to handle all different kinds of people because you know how to make them feel good. We all have a social need, and as we raise our emotional intelligence we become better at building and keeping relationships that help us satisfy that need. We make ourselves feel better and we raise our self-esteem by helping others feel good.

To raise your emotional intelligence you simply have to listen to yourself more often. Take a break and ask your body what it is feeling. Do you feel some tension or pain anywhere? Listen to your intuition (your gut feeling). As soon as you open up to the information that is already within you, you will find out that you "know" much more than you were aware of before.

Do not ignore or try to push emotions away. They have something important to tell you. Your emotions will help you to raise your self-esteem. Many people with low self-esteem try to ignore their negative emotions. They may have learnt through their childhoods that negative emotions are bad and should not be expressed, or they may simply not know how to handle their emotions. People with low self-esteem often translate having negative emotions into being a bad person. They assume that if they are feeling sad, angry or scared it must be because they are either doing something wrong or they do not deserve to feel differently. People with high self-esteem pay attention and are sensitive to their emotions without ignoring them or sweeping them aside. They do not equate feeling bad with being bad. They handle negative feelings in a positive manner. People with high self-esteem learn from their negative emotions and take active steps to make themselves feel better (for example by making sure that they get their unfulfilled needs met).

To keep your self-esteem high you thus have to accept your emotions. Ask yourself what you need in order to heal your wound or to find better balance. If you need social support, ask for it! If you need to slow down and relax, do it! You may simply need to have a good cry to offload some pressure, and everything will be fine again. Welcome your emotions and listen to what they are trying to tell you!

How to Improve Your Emotional Intelligence

1. Identify your own emotion at the time you are exhibiting it or shortly thereafter and name it. (Anger, frustration, joy, grief, abandonment, fear, love, confusion, etc.)

2. Identify what caused the emotion. (Memory from the past, friction with a disrespected colleague, threat of looking bad.)

3. Accept the emotion and what it has meant to your emotional development. (Is there a pattern? Are you perceived as eruptive, self-centered etc.?)

4. Express the named emotion and the cause to whoever is witnessing it or to someone else appropriate. (This may include an apology, an explanation,

a compliment, etc.)

If you feel that others have a pre-conceived negative opinion of you, you may ask them how you are being perceived. If you don't want to do that, build your own self-awareness by quickly naming your emotions as they develop, identify what causes them, accepting them and expressing them to someone. Only then will you be able to catch yourself and project in a calmer more collective manner as opposed to exhibiting predictable negative behavior. Decreasing the negative behavior will help to reform opinions from colleagues.

If you are able to identify and control your own emotions with practice, then you are ready to put those skills to use for your team whenever there is a conflict or need for change. For individuals to work together they must build bridges across perspectives with compassion. Compassion is not agreement. It is a consideration for another person's feelings and is essential on teams before two objecting parties' lapse into defensiveness and a toxic work environment ensues.

Emotional Intelligence With Your Colleagues.

1. Ask yourself what you need to stop doing to make the team work effectively.

2. Be curious and compassionate to the others' perspectives. Learn to view things from their angle too. Be a good listener ask questions. Articulate what you understand their point of view to be. Use "I" statements and not "you" statements.

3. Use the steps above to understand the emotions and behaviors of others.

4. Make a suggestion as to how the conflict may be handled with compassion to all parties.

Identify the ideal self, In a way, this is analogous to imagining the future state of an organization - what it would look like without defects, rework, misalignment of work and requirements, etc. - but the ideal self is much more personal. One person's ideal self, building on his or her core identity and aspirations, will be different from another's ideal self. Personal change starts with envisioning the ideal self - the way one would like to be, to work, and to be perceived, but this is much more personal. This has three elements:

Awareness Of One's Strengths

An image of the desired future and a sense of hope that the desired future is attainable Insight into the ideal self are not always straightforward. One might simply extrapolate a trend of the present instead of envisioning a truly desired future self. Talking about aspirations with trusted friends or mentors can help. But identifying a clear picture of the future self-one wishes to be is a foundational step in Intentional Change Theory.

Identify the real self is not as easy as it sounds. In "Primal Leadership" Goleman, Boyatzis, and McKee report, "We found that an alarming number of leaders do not really know if they have resonance with their organizations. Rather they suffer from CEO disease; it's one unpleasant symptom is the sufferer's near-total ignorance about how his mood and actions appear to the organization. It's not that leaders don't care how they are perceived; most do. But they incorrectly assume that they can decipher this information themselves. Worse, they think that if they are having a negative effect, someone will tell them. They're wrong." The greatest challenge is to see oneself as others do. Using multiple sources of feedback can be very useful. Many organizations use 360 reviews for all individuals in management positions. However, the self-assessments are customarily inflated because it is the start of negotiation position. [Boyatzis uses 360 reviews to measure the correlation between EQ and operating results, but he says they throw away the self-assessments as "they are largely delusional."] Identification of the actual self requires honest and objective feedback. Behavioral feedback (such as video) and psychological tests can also help.

Develop a learning agenda, come up with an agenda and plan in contrast to the stream of to-dos and complying with agendas of others, the learning agenda is development focused. In Leadership Development from a Complexity Perspective, Boyatzis says that "a person often needs a type of permission to let go of old habits and try new ones." A learning agenda provides that type of structure for exploration and learning. The fourth step is Experimentation and Practice, look for feedback, and practice again. A consultant, coach or mentor should help the individual who has embarked on intentional change to find safe settings to practice the characteristics of the effective leader he or she envisions. Finally build Helping relationships, someone whose experience you can learn from. People like Coaches, mentors, guides are very helpful to someone aiming to transition to the ideal self through practicing greater EQ and inspirational leadership.

HOW TO USE THE ABCDE THEORY OF EMOTIONS

The ABCDE model is a model that makes it necessary for each stage be completed before advancing to the next stage. During moments of low emotional intelligence the ABCDE model is a useful tool to help employees reach a resolution. Let us take a closer look at each stage of the ABCDE model and how it's been used by coaches to groom people into becoming better emotional beings.

ABCDE Model

A = Activating event

B = Belief system

C = Emotional Consequences of A and B

D = Disputing irrational thoughts and beliefs.

E = Cognitive and Emotional effects of "updated" beliefs

Activating Event/Situation: The activating stage involves a triggering occurrence or situation and coming to terms with the negative feelings and emotions that are related to the event. It is important to look closely at the automatic thoughts - those thoughts that have an immediate reaction to an experience. It is helpful to put down these thoughts and feelings associated with the event in writing. This stage must be completed before moving on to stage

Belief System: the second stage is the belief stage, in this stage a coach guides the employee to recognize that beliefs trigger negative automatic thoughts. This is significant because thoughts ultimately determine the actions that are taken. Beliefs are formed throughout a person's life, from childhood on, and need to be analyzed in order to change those beliefs that cause negative thoughts and actions.

Emotional Consequences: This stage involves discussing the internal and external trait that followed as a result of an employee's beliefs and situation. The internal consequences are those emotions felt inside such as a change in heart rate or stomach butterflies. External consequences are the behaviors exhibited such as yelling at another person or slamming a door when exiting a room. As in all stages, this must be completed before progressing to the next step.

Dispute: In stage 4 thoughts and beliefs now at a disputed to cross check if they are rational or irrational. If they are worth it or not should and must beliefs that seem concrete and do not allow flexibility need to be disputed for validity. For example, if a belief that all employees must be nice to each other is held, during this stage it will be disputed to determine if this belief is true.

When looking at the Dispute stage there are three key kinds of disputes that can be used:

Scientific dispute – Are there any proof to the claims or basis for the belief, feelings, or thought pattern

Functional dispute – Is the belief supporting some other, potentially unconscious goals?

Logical dispute – Does the belief system make common sense? Is there any generalization or other thought pattern influencing these beliefs?

Example: A person who recognizes the thought pattern and changes and sees they are not based on truth or logic and adapts over the time to a view of believing that they can do a better job at expressing his beliefs.

Exchange: In this final stage, beliefs that have been disputed and determined as irrational are exchanged for beliefs that are rational. Replacing negative beliefs that cause negative thoughts is necessary to reframe an employee's thinking for the future. Changing beliefs, thought patterns and actions does not occur over night. But once the new, positive beliefs and thoughts have been identified, they can be written down and referenced as often as necessary until they become automatic thoughts.

The ABCDE Model of coaching is a great tool that HR managers can use in the workplace to assist developing higher emotional intelligence level in employees. As a result of systematic CBC conferences, employees experiencing instances of low emotional intelligence can be led to have healthy automatic thoughts that will equip them to make wise decisions and produce positive consequences.

Emotional Contagion And Empathy

Emotional contagion in its most positive form is the basis of the human virtue of empathy. We need to be emotionally in tune with others in order to understand them, get along with them and to function effectively in the human social world. Highly sensitive people's finely detailed observational abilities make them more responsive than most to the nuances of other people's feelings. This sometimes leads them to shy away from crowds since the mass of emotional messages is just too confusing. But even one-on-one relating can be emotionally challenging to a person who reads and responds strongly other's subtle emotional cues. Since HSP's own emotional responses are intense, quick to arise and hard to shake off, they often find themselves getting caught up uncomfortably in other people's feelings. Being attuned to the rawness of other people's emotions and even taking them on through emotional contagion can be an unpleasant and aversive experience.

Danger Of Co-Dependency

Since vicariously experiencing others unhappiness, rage or despair are so painful for a highly sensitive individual, it is easy to understand why it would be tempting for them to collude or manage social situations so as to keep others on an emotionally even keel. When the need to ensure that those around them are never angry or upset becomes a preoccupation there is a danger of developing co-dependent relationships.

MASTERY OF EMOTION:
A KEY TO A BETTER LIFE

To live a better and happier life, you must take charge of the natural instinctive state of your mind arising from circumstances, moods or relationships with others. Controlling your emotions doesn't mean ignoring them, it means you recognize and take rightful actions on them. You must be in-charge of your emotions day-to-day! If you truly desire unlimited happiness, you must control your emotions. Do you struggle to control your emotions? You have the power to create your state of blissful and favorable emotional circumstances. A clear mind is better and able to control emotions. Un-clutter your mind!

Emotion is the generic term for subjective or conscious experience that is characterized by psycho-physiological expressions, biological reactions and mental states. It is often associated and considered reciprocally influential with temperament, personality, mood, motivation and depression. Emotions can be influenced by hormones and alcohol. It is the force behind human actions and reactions. Emotions can be expressed in the form of fear, joy, envy, excitement, distrust, depression, curiosity, contentment, desire, despair, embarrassment, confidence, gratitude, happiness, shame and shock.

With the harsh weather conditions, the economy in a miserable state, lack of job security, infidel partner, stubborn children, nagging co-workers, and unrest in the society, it can be easy to allow your emotions to run amok. An uncontrolled state of mind can make a bad situation worse. Every emotion begins with a thought. If you learn to control your mind and thoughts, you can rule your emotions. Guard your heart because out of it flows the issues of life. As you think in your heart, so you are. While it does take practice, you can be in firm control of any of the particular feelings that characterize the state of your mind, such as hate, horror, anger, fear, happiness or love.

Learning to control your emotions during challenging times of emotional stress is beneficial to your mental and general health. Emotions play a great role in life, and decisions are often based on feelings. However, problems occur when emotions are out of control. Becoming a master of emotional intelligence which involves emotional literacy, emotional coping and emotional awareness will help improve your emotional sagacity which helps you develop a good emotional freedom technique. To go higher in your career, build good relationships with people and be successful in life, you must keep a tab on your emotional quotient. It is common in day-to-day life to regret those actions we took because of uncontrolled emotion. There are keys that will help you lead a healthy and better emotional state in life.

1. Recognize Your Emotions

Human feelings are expressed in different forms. Take time to understand the nature of your feelings. Some of the most difficult emotions include anger, depression, anxiety and fear; the good News is that they can be subdued.

2. Meditation

The best way to maintain a good emotional health is to focus and dwell on uplifting and empowering thoughts. This will help you harmonize your mind, spirit and body. Meditation helps you to be in-charge of your physical, mental and emotional health. Some people meditate using prayer, yoga, reading a life-enriching book or listening to soul-uplifting music.

3. Affirmation

Affirmation is like confirmation. Through this means you speak faith into your circumstances and gladly expect the best result with cheerful expectancy. Say to yourself, "Am a success." "Am favored beyond measure and things are falling in pleasant places for me." This kind of positive thinking and confessions can change your mood from bad to good.

Over 80% of the things we worry about never happen and 15% out of the other 20% of the time, things don't happen as bad as we thought. Worrying only saps you of energy and vitality. These keys listed above can help you develop your cope capacity, create and be in-charge of your favorable emotional state 24/7. You can handle situations more than you ever thought possible by taking full control of your emotion in your day-to-day life.

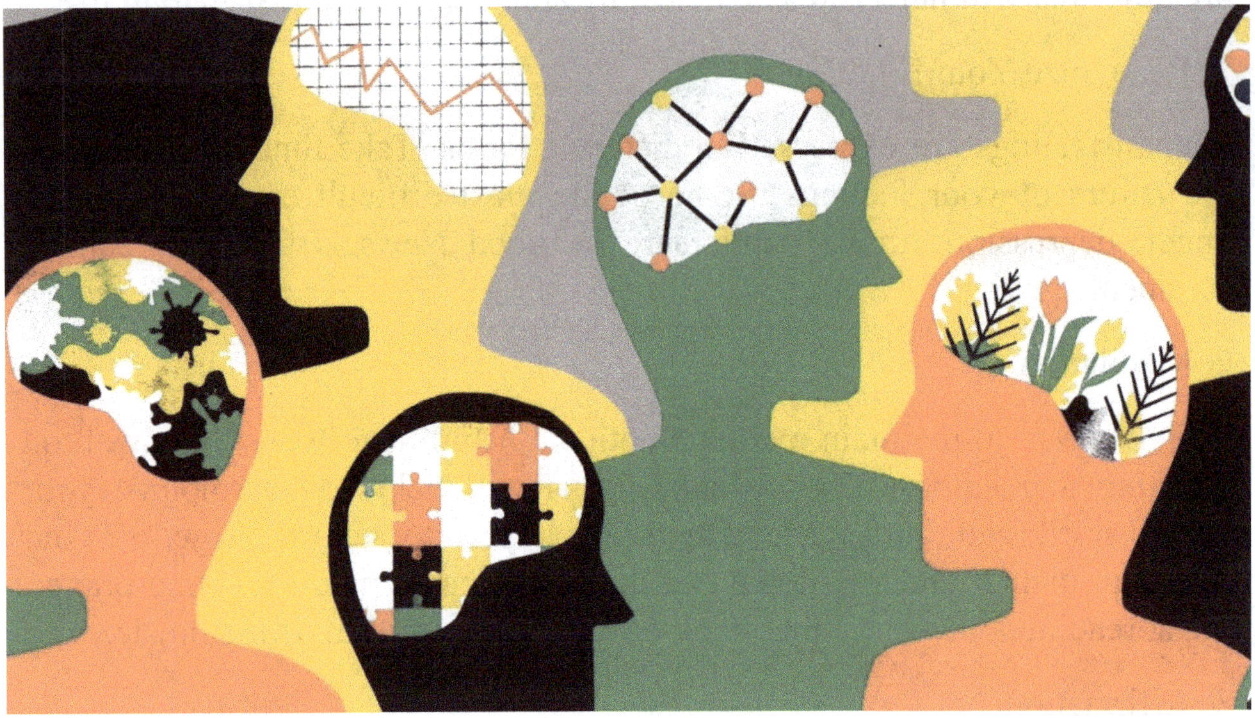

GROWING EMOTIONAL INTELLIGENCE

So, what can you do about this? How can you turn this around and begin to grow your Emotional Intelligence?

A first step is to pay more attention to your emotions by noticing their sensations in your body. Before reaching for the TV remote, that sugary snack, caffeine, alcohol, or painkillers, notice the sensations of emotion.

Ask yourself, "If this feeling were located somewhere in my body where that would be?" Then, describe it as a physical sensation. Is it hot, cold? Is there tightness or pressure? Numbness? Tingling? Itching? Nausea? Expansion? Contraction? Rising? Sinking?

While noticing these sensations, especially if they feel uncomfortable, may seem like an odd thing to do to be happier, it's a first step toward connecting with emotional guidance. There's a deeper wisdom nudging you in these sensations. Paying attention to the sensations of emotions is a way to access them, observe them, and allow them to inform you.

Once you are in touch with the sensation, ask yourself, "What is the message in this emotion?" Just notice what comes to mind.

If you're hesitant to engage with emotions, it's important to keep in mind that emotions are transient. No feeling lasts forever. They arise with a purpose. While present, an emotion gives you information about what is going on inside you, around you, and with others-along with energy to do something about it. Once emotional guidance is heeded, it subsides.

How Does Emotional Intelligence Affect Your Life?

Performance at work - EQ helps you to comfortably handle social complexities of workplace, motivate and guide others and succeed in your career. Now-a-days companies view emotional intelligence as being an important aspect and perform EQ testing before hiring.

Physical well-being - Stress is imminent in today's world no matter which profession you belong to. Stress is a familiar factor leading to serious health issues in most of the people. Uncontrolled stress level is known to increase the risk of heart disease. Our immune system suffers when stress level are high.

Mental well-being - Stress affects mental health negatively. You might have read or heard about stressed people going to the extent of committing suicide. When you cannot manage your emotions you become a victim of mood swings or other mental disorders that can seldom allow you to form or maintain strong relationships in life.

Personal relationships - Understanding your emotions help you to express your feelings to your loved ones. When there is a block in communication your relationships suffer both at work and in your personal life.

Improving Communication

If you want to improve your communication skills, it may be easier than you think! It is generally accepted that communication is the skill of both talking and listening, however, there are other more subtle ways to communicate, which can sometimes let us down. Body language and non-verbal cues such as facial expressions and hand gestures all have their place in good communications.

Most people who want to improve their communication skills do so because of their perception of themselves. They may be shy at parties, unwilling to participate in meetings, or feel they have nothing to say at social gatherings.

Yet those same people can often talk the hind legs off a donkey if they are able to discuss a subject close to them - better still if they are in their own home. This all comes down to confidence.

The simplest way to develop the confidence to talk freely at a social event is to pursue a popular pastime, sport or hobby that involves other people. While stamp collecting is fine, unless you happen to be in the same room at the same time as a fellow enthusiast, you'll struggle to make an impression. However, if you opt for let's say, learning a musical instrument, or playing any sport, you will be able to engage people's interest even if you're playing the guitar and they're playing piano. So making good conversation is not necessarily about having the same passions as everybody else - you just have to have a passion for something.

Being a good communicator can also help advance your working career. If you walk into the boss's office staring at your shoes, and mumbling about the pay rise that you deserve, you won't get far. However, if you enter the office with your head held high and your shoulders back, speaking clearly and decisively, you may actually walk out with a bigger raise than you were hoping to achieve.

Changing Negative Emotions

Negativity exists in our lives. There is no way around it. No matter how hard you try to live in the moment, focus on positivity, or practice being grateful every day, you will still experience times of negative emotions in your life. But this can be a good thing. Negative emotions signal that you need to make a change in your life. Whether it is stress, anger, fear, jealously, resentment, or any other negative emotion, the point of them all is to warn you that something needs to change.

Negative Emotions Are Our Number And To Transfer Negative Emotion We Need To :

1.) Change your energy field. Close your eyes and imagine the emotion as energy around you. What does it look like, what color, shape, form etc. does it take? Now allow it to change and smooth out, becoming transformed, harmonized, peaceful. What does it look and feel like now?

2.) Change your perspective on the situation. Re-frame it in a way that's positive/productive for you. Ask yourself, how this situation can help you. What is good about it? How are you growing from it? A positive attitude about something can help resolve it for you, even if it's a difficult situation. A new mindset can change everything.

3.) Ask self what the lesson you are learning from this situation is. Knowing the lesson helps transform the negative feeling and take on the mastery of the lesson you are in the process of learning.

4.) Put a new and positive picture in your mind about the situation that is causing the hurtful emotion. Instead of dwelling on the painful scenario or the trauma incident or being yelled at or treated disrespectfully, replace it with one of yourself healed, happy, successful, determined to move on etc. Whatever feels great and counters the old feeling. Keep the new picture in place whenever the old feeling comes up. The mind and body respond quickly to pictures, so this will shift you fast.

5.) Inner Listening. Get very quiet and go into the silence within. Allow your inner guide to bring you new insights, wisdom and solutions for healing and transformation.

6.) Forgiveness means letting go. It doesn't condone bad behavior, but lets the pain go. You and others have the right to make mistakes and grow. Forgive self if needed and forgive others. This doesn't mean that you will choose to stay connected with anyone who harms you. It means you let go of the painful movie, get the lesson and move forward. You stop the images and negative emotions from their endless control over you. Restore your self- esteem if you've acted poorly and wish the other person well if they have. To clean yourself completely, do a systematic of forgiveness for everyone in your life. You will be rejuvenated. Forgive; let go and say goodbye to these emotions.

7.) Change a gripe to a goal. If you regularly complain and feel negatively about something or someone, set a goal for yourself and be determined to accomplish it. For example, if you are jealous of someone who has a degree in art; stop it and find a way to get one for yourself. If you are short of money and angry at others who have it, stop it and chart your path, make a plan to increase your income. Things happen first in the mind, so begin to visualize yourself having what you want already now. Feel the joy of it and for 5 minutes several times a day, sit quietly and feel the emotions you would have if it were yours now. Soon you begin to believe you have it. In the Biology of belief, Bruce Lipton offers scientific proof that we get what we believe.

8.) Thoughts and emotions are intimately connected in fact, inseparable. One leads to the other. What repetitive thoughts do you have that are hurting you? Are you taking charge of your negative thoughts and transforming them? Think the opposite of your negative thought as soon as you catch yourself having it. Correct yourself on a daily basis; over and over. Repetition of the new corrected thought forges a new brain pathway and pattern. Strong intention and follow through is necessary.

Don't let your mind wander all day without direction or self-monitoring. You can change your mind at any moment into a more positive state. Letting your thoughts run wild will take away your peace. Take charge of yourself and choose thoughts that will help you.

9.) What belief about yourself do you want to change

Finances, relationships, self-concept, accomplishment of a specific goal; health, personal qualities etc. Beliefs that limit and cause pain keep your emotions at a painful level, and only you can change that.

Taking Positive New Action

1) Set clear boundaries. You decide what you will and won't accept from people and act on it.

2) Practice assertive communication with others. Tell them how you feel without blame or judgment; just how you feel. Stand up for self if needed.

3) Be creative. Create something positive from your experience.

For example, women who have been abused have set up women's shelters around the country. People who grew up hungry have started programs to feed poor children.

All of these techniques work. Practice and practice and you will see yourself and your life become fulfilled and beautiful. Be very patient with yourself, as this is hard work and takes a lot of self- control, intention and discipline. It's a progressive unfolding of the highest part of self. Over time we blossom!

Steps in Review:

1.) Stop and control self.

2.) Release the emotion.

3.) Transform the emotion.

4.) Take positive new action.

5.) Replace negative emotional reactions with spiritual actions and personal spiritual qualities.

Change your life by taking control of your emotions instead of being taken over by them and held in their grip.

Acknowledge That the Negativity Is A Sign

The first thing you need to do is actually sit down and acknowledge that you are in a negative space. Maybe you've just been dumped and are feeling sad, or maybe you are stressed out and resenting your job. It is OK to feel this way. In fact, it's normal!

Sometimes bad things happen that impact our lives in negative ways. The oft-used phrase "shit happens" nails it on the head. Shit really does happen, and it is fine to experience some negative emotions when it does. The important part is what you choose to do next. Once you have accepted your negative emotions you need to acknowledge that they are a sign that something needs to change. Do not ignore them. You are feeling that way for a reason. It is time to make some positive changes!

Figure Out What Action Is Required

Now that you are at one with the idea that some change is required in your life you need to figure out what that actual change is. What are your emotions telling you to do? It's normally pretty obvious. Are you stressed in your job? Find a new one. Hating your relationship? End it. Bored with life? Sell everything and take a holiday. Well it might not be that simple as this but I can assure you that it is pretty simple. You can go a little deeper by assessing exactly what is negative about your current situation. Try to break it down to the smallest possible level.

For example, once you start doing this you might realize that your job really isn't that stressful normally but it is just this one project that is killing you. So now you know that you only need to fix your current workload and you actually don't need to quit your job, sell your things, and go live in a cave as a hermit. Phew.

Take a step

This is the hard part. Acknowledging the negativity and figuring out what action is required is easy most of the time. Actually doing something about it is where most people will encounter trouble. The biggest blocker to taking action is a fear of change. People are often scared of change because they do not know exactly what is going to happen once the change occurs. Well I've got news for you - the future is constantly changing and you will never ever know exactly what is going to happen. Never!

The very definition of the future means that it a step forward in time which means that things have changed. Time has progressed and billions of actions have taken place. And this occurs every second! You cannot stop the change process because but you can make sure that in your life you are the one in control of the changes. Inaction and indecision are common symptoms of a fear of change (and fear of failure/success). By not taking action you let everyone else in the world decide what will happen for your life. You give away your power and become helpless. But if you choose to be decisive and start taking action you begin creating the changes that you want instead of being inundated by the changes that everyone else wants.

Keep Adjusting

You won't get it right first time but you will learn a hell of a lot along the way. Maybe the first change you made was not enough. Maybe you really did hate your job after all and just fixing that one project didn't help. So you readjust. You take stock again, assess the situation, and make another change. Another positive change that is. Or maybe the first change you made was too drastic and you realize that the original situation was better than the one you are in now. That's fine too. Just readjust and try again until you get it right and find a place where you feel happy, excited, and passionate.

Delete Negating Emotions From Your System

There is nothing beautiful about negative emotions; it's an obstacle to living a well-deserved life. despite the fact that life doesn't always turn out the way we expect we must keep a check on our emotions and not allow circumstances decide how we live our life .Negative emotions, across the board, could be reduced and the cumulative effects of the emotions from all spiritual experiences could be deleted-just like you delete things from a computer's hard drive. Essentially, we would then have less negative emotion to ruin us. And when we have one new emotion, it would not trigger all the previous old emotions in combination with each other.

In the case of a mother, for example, worrying about her child's welfare is not going to change anything for the better. In fact, the mother worrying about the child's health will actually make the condition worse for the child, so the worries have to be reduced or pretty much deleted. There should be no worries, no negative thoughts and no negative emotions about a child.

It's not about suppressing, repressing or denying the negative emotions and negative thoughts. Nor does it work to numb yourself out or try to forget about them. These emotions and thoughts should be truthfully deleted, so they can't come back and haunt the situation. If left undeleted, negative emotions can cause a continuous struggle throughout your entire life-not only your life, but the lives of those around you.

You can learn the skill needed to delete emotions for yourself and others. In order to delete the emotion of sadness, for example, you could just get in touch with one thing in your life that makes you feel the emotion of sadness. This establishes a baseline that you can check into later in order to feel the change.

Essentially, all you do is put some thought energy on your midline while deleting the cumulative effect of all the sadness in your spiritual experiences. There is a three stage deletion process to this protocol, but after you experience the process, it would become more automatic and almost instantaneous. This is a good skill to learn for everyone.

CONCLUSION

Paying attention to your emotion is the first step to becoming a master of emotional intelligence, emotions are inborn and we have seen through the course of this book that emotions can be found in humans as well as in animals in the form of empathy, we see that animals are able to relate with their owners during times of distress, pain sorry, fear we see that some behaviors like adaptability allows an individual to understand the emotions or motives of others and as a result they are more willing to adapt to a situation than a person who can only understand what they personally are feeling. We come to realize that empathy is the highest level of communication skill and it should be put to use more often as it allows one to relate well with peoples unspoken words and the feelings created by them in others. Empathy is also responsible for how we respond to other's feelings sympathetically so that they can win their trust, which promotes communication further. Our fear of failure, anger, and frustration suddenly drop away, allowing for a more meaningful dialogue and a deepening of relationships, we are finally able to feel what others feel and skills like emotional control helps the individual control their emotions when they try to go overboard . During times of stress emotional intelligence plays a great role as they are able to find a way around it, they are optimistic and are good at building strong relationships. We also learnt that being a good communicator can also help advance your working career, improve relationship between employee and boss; EI and EQ are useful for human relations as they help clients decide

Developing these skills takes a lot of time, even years. But a little conscious effort can reduce this time down to a fraction of how long it would ordinarily take. The journey to mastering emotional intelligence is not for individuals who are ready to make a difference in life and make things work out for them as they climb up the ladder of success. You can Change your life by taking charge of your emotions rather of being taken over by them and held in their grip. One must remember that emotions are powerful but we decide what gets to us. Mastery will be within our reach once we are able to acknowledge the benefits of emotional intelligence to our lives. Remember to acknowledge That Negativity Is A Sign , then try to figure Out What Action Is Required to make this problem go away , then take the necessary actions.

EMPATHY

© **Copyright 2021 - All rights reserved.**

The content contained within this book may not be reproduced, duplicated or transmitted without direct written permission from the author or the publisher.

Under no circumstances will any blame or legal responsibility be held against the publisher, or author, for any damages, reparation, or monetary loss due to the information contained within this book. Either directly or indirectly.

Legal Notice:

This book is copyright protected. This book is only for personal use. You cannot amend, distribute, sell, use, quote or paraphrase any part, or the content within this book, without the consent of the author or publisher.

Disclaimer Notice:

Please note the information contained within this document is for educational and entertainment purposes only. All effort has been executed to present accurate, up to date, and reliable, complete information. No warranties of any kind are declared or implied. Readers acknowledge that the author is not engaging in the rendering of legal, financial, medical or professional advice. The content within this book has been derived from various sources. Please consult a licensed professional before attempting any techniques outlined in this book.

By reading this document, the reader agrees that under no circumstances is the author responsible for any losses, direct or indirect, which are incurred as a result of the use of information contained within this document, including, but not limited to, — errors, omissions, or inaccuracies.

TABLE OF CONTENT

CHAPTER 1: UNDERSTANDING AN EMPATH
- Who Is an Empath?
- Are You An Empath?
- How to Tell If You Are An Empath
- Characteristics of an Empath
- 20 Things That Might Mean You Are an Empath
- Empaths - The Sensitive Ones

CHAPTER 2: HIGHLY SENSITIVE PEOPLE
- Highly Sensitive People
- Highly Sensitive People -- An Introduction to the Trait of High Sensitivity
- Highly Sensitive People - Sounds, Smells and Sentiments
- Highly Sensitive People Traits and Characteristics
- Ten Ways to Tell If You Are an Extra Sensitive Person
- The Emotional Rollercoaster of Empaths and Highly Sensitive People
- Understanding Highly Sensitive People
- 5 Myths about Highly Sensitive People

CHAPTER 3: EMPHATIC ABILITIES
- Empathic Psychic Abilities - Do You Possess This Type of Psychic Ability?
- Empathic Psychic Abilities - Psychic Guide
- Empathic Abilities - What Are They and How to Tell If You Have Them
- Becoming the Ultimate Empathizer
- How to Empathize with Your Partner Better
- How to Empathize with Others in 3 Simple Steps
- The Power of Empathic Listening
- Learn to Develop Empathic Listening
- Empathic Shielding

CHAPTER 4: GUIDE ON HOW TO OVERCOME FEAR
- Fear Factor
- Overcome Fear and Overcome Your Fate
- Controlling Your Mind: How to Overcome Fear
- A Guide to Overcoming Stress, Anxiety and Depression
- Face-To-Face With Your Fear and Anxiety
- 7 Tips in Having the Right Mindset to Overcome Fear
- Overcoming Fears with Psychic Abilities

CHAPTER 5: SURVIVAL GUIDE FOR EMPHATIC AND HIGHLY SENSITIVE PEOPLE
- Emotional Intelligence and the Empathic Spirit
- Resources for Empaths and Emotionally Sensitive People

[4 Steps to Turn Your Sensitivity into Your Superpower](#)
[9 Tips for the Spiritually Sensitive and Empaths](#)
[A Survival Guide for Empaths and Highly Sensitive Persons](#)

CHAPTER 1

UNDERSTANDING AN EMPATH

Who Is an Empath?

What does it mean to be an "empath"? Does it mean I'm psychic? Or does it simply mean that I'm incredibly sensitive to the emotional feelings of others? Are empaths more likely to be really "good" people? Do they have any other natural gifts or sensitivities that are noteworthy? And how do empaths USE their gifts in the real world to make a difference or an impact in the places that they live?

Describing what an empath IS...is quite simple:

An empath is someone who has an unusually strong sense of connection, sensitivity and "simpatico' with the emotions and feelings of other people. The word sensitive is probably the word that conveys the essence of what an empath IS, better than any other word...however, it doesn't mean they are emotionally sensitive themselves.

In other words, many empaths are very practical and pragmatic with their own emotions but are highly sensitive to YOURS.

Are all empaths naturally really good people?

It's a funny question and one that probably can't be answered with 100% carte blanche certainty as a result. BUT, in my own experience, empaths tend to be highly caring, nurturing and emotionally available people by nature, and tend to be givers, rather than takers as a general rule as well.

What kind of work do empaths do?

The most common is service work that incorporates their gifts in a way that "serves" the people who need them most.

For example?

Many empaths have tremendous psychic and intuitive gifts, simply because they are far more naturally connected to the emotions and needs of other people. Many social scientists describe empaths as having a very REAL "6th sense" which is the ability to identify, understand and ultimately bond with people and their problems in the way that most of us can't. This leads to an astounding amount of insight and intuition that can border on being unexplained.

Some recent studies seem to suggest that the 6th sense that emotional empaths have is quite literally, a more highly developed brain in 2 specific areas.

What are they?

The area in the brain that modulates a feeling of "connection" to others, (well known to be triggered through meditation) and another area deep in the brain thought to trigger synesthesia, a little known but proven phenomena where people can hear colours and see sounds. (it's also thought by many to be a possible scientific explanation for everything from psychic abilities to spirit communication to seeing and sensing auras)

Are all empaths psychic?

Not. But MANY, inexplicably... are. And when you combine these two little-understood abilities, you get people who not only are incredibly attuned to the energetic frequencies of others; they are ALSO able to see future events and make powerful predictions about how where you are NOW will impact where you're going to end up. (and what you MAY need to do to avoid a catastrophe before you get there!)

The power of an empath is not always seen as important as it should be. Those with the skills of an empath maintain psychic abilities which could prove enormously helpful to those dealing with serious psychological issues. How is this so? An empath has the potential to perform emotional healing which can be considered a tremendous benefit to those suffering from depression and other related mental issues.

The reason this is so is that an empath is an individual that can "feel" the emotions of another person. This does not just refer to the ability to be perceptive to someone's emotional state. Such talents can be considered a skill, but it would hardly rise to the level of psychic ability. No, with an empath, the sensitivity to a person's emotional state will be far deeper and far more impactful. An empath can tap into the emotional aura of a person and outright experience what the other person is feeling.

In essence, the empath will extract a duplication of the other person's emotions and absorb them into his/her being. Once these emotions have been absorbed, the empath becomes the other person at least from an emotionally perceptive state. In many ways, this can be one of the most difficult of all psychic abilities to endure. It can be a sincerely troubling thing to deal with one's emotional state much less that of another person. The empath will do so and experience exactly what another is experiencing.

Questions will arise regarding why an empath would do this. Different empaths have different reason and motivations for their actions. One reason that people cultivate their abilities to serve as an empath would be to act as an emotional healer. Yes, it is possible to enter into the mind and psyche of the person whose emotions are being fused with and reducing the negative energy and replacing it with positive energy. This can yield a unique response in the form of eradicating the negative psychological holds poor energy can have on a person. And in some cases, the negative psychological consequences can be reversed or outright eliminated. That is certainly a good thing and the results of which could free a person of problematic psychic hindrances forever more.

This is not to suggest that meeting with an empath will automatically replace the need for seeking the help of a legitimate psychotherapist. The level of one's psychological dysfunction must always be addressed when discussing whether or not an empath should be the primary caregiver. In some instances, serious psychiatric help may be required. However, there is no reason why an empath cannot offer secondary help to those in dire need of it. The secondary help offered by the empath could prove to be a tremendous support to even the most serious of all psychological conditions.

A discussion about the psychic abilities of an empath is far more complex than more people realize. An empath is more than just a perceptive person. Rather, the empath can be considered an emotional chameleon that is capable of delving deep into the emotional state of another. In some cases, the empath may even determine the process for healing even the most afflicted emotional energy.

Are You An Empath?

Empathic people are emotionally sensitive. In these changing times, people who have always been sensitive may find they are even more sensitive now. And people who were not that sensitive may find they are becoming more so.

According to Dr Kyra Mesich, sensitivity is an issue of our times. And for the reasons stated above I agree. It impacts all types of personalities, ages, cultures. It is especially prevalent in people who try to impact other people positively.

It is more often activated in situations with people who mirror our subconscious feelings and beliefs.

Why should you care about this? Well first of all, if you are not aware of it, it can explain certain phenomena happening in your life that you may not have understood before such as unexplained mood swings such as crying for no apparent reason or very angry about something that might normally just be an irritant, increased fatigue, insomnia, body aches and tension, and illness... also could be buoyantly happy..

From a business or career perspective, it can impact your ability to be productive, interact with others, make a contribution in the world and have the energy to make a good living doing it. From a personal standpoint, it can impact your ability to have fun, partake in physical activity, your relationships and your well-being. And that's just a start.

What are the signs that you are an empath?

(emotionally sensitive)

1. Emotionally sensitive people feel emotions often and deeply. They may feel as if they "wear their emotions on their sleeves but not necessarily. Men may feel things but not show it as much due to cultural training that it is not okay to do so.

2. They are keenly aware of the emotions of people around them.

3. Sensitive people are easily hurt or upset. An insult or unkind remark will affect them deeply.

4. In a similar vein, sensitive people may strive to avoid conflicts because the negativity affects them so much.

5. Sensitive people are not able to shake off emotions easily. Once they are saddened or upset by something, they cannot just switch gears and forget it. (this appears to be changing)

6. Sensitive people are greatly affected by emotions they witness. They feel deeply for others' suffering. They may cry at Hallmark commercials or when others cry or when they connect deeply with someone.

7. Sensitive people may suffer from recurrent depression, anxiety or other psychological disorders.

8. On the positive side, sensitive people, are also keenly aware of and affected by beauty in art, music and nature. They are the world's greatest artists and art appreciators.

9. Sensitive people are prone to stimulus overload. That is, they can't stand large crowds, loud noise, or hectic environments. They feel overwhelmed and depleted by too many stimuli.

10. Sensitive people are born that way. They were sensitive children. I think this is not as true as it once was. As I said before, people are becoming more sensitive than they ever were.

11. A truly sensitive person sometimes feels animosity toward his sensitive nature. Most sensitive people whole-heartedly wish they were tougher and more thick-skinned. They feel like their sensitivity is a weakness. Therefore some sensitive adults have learned how to hide their sensitivity from others.

How to Tell If You Are An Empath

Are you an Empath? If you answer yes to some of the following questions, you probably are:

• I can tell when someone says one thing but means another.

• I can often see through other peoples' eyes.

• I get compliments like: "You understand me better than others do."

• If I have to give the same speech to three different strangers, it comes out differently every time. Somehow I sense the way they need to hear the information.

• I can easily feel the negative emotions and physical symptoms of another.

• I feel particularly free when outside in nature.

• I can easily connect with my pet's world.

• Watching TV shows with highly dramatic emotional confrontations like Jerry Springer makes me feel sick and cry.

• My friendships are much more intense than others' friendships.

• My need to connect with others like myself is strong, to know I'm not alone.

Empaths can be people pleasers. It is so easy for them to know what others want to hear and to have. They tend to be kind people who only want to help. Often they are found in the helping professions like healers and caregivers. They volunteer their time and energy and think nothing of giving all they have, sometimes to their detriment.

It is important for Empaths to take time for themselves. Because they give away so much of their energy or it is drawn from them, they need to find a quiet place to recharge. Consider using some protection images every day to keep others from draining your energy, particularly in crowded places like buses, subways and stores. The elderly and young mothers will draw energy from you without meaning to.

Being an Empath is not a choice. Either you were born that way or not. That means that you may have been receiving other people's energies from day one. Like when my father was in the hospital having his gall bladder removed, I could feel my mother's worry about him for days afterwards. And when my dear grandfather died when I was eight years old, I have memories of my mother's overwhelming grief and sadness that I thought were my emotions.

Most of the clients I see have some empathic ability and don't know it. When they feel bad, which is often, they believe it is their own emotions causing this. A lot of the time they have picked up a negative emotion like fear, anger or sadness from someone close to them and cannot tell that it is not their own. That is quite understandable if you don't know that is something you could do.

Here is a little exercise to recognize which emotions are yours. When you get comfortable doing this, you will be able to tell when you have picked up emotions that are not yours.

Is This Mine?

1. Take three slow deep breaths;

2. One at a time, pay attention:

- To your breath

- To your physical body

- To your conscious mind

- To your emotions right now

3. Notice how the above four feel right now.

When you notice something different happening in one of the above four through your day, try the following ways to Release:

1. Say, "All that does not belong to me, be gone;"

2. In your mind cut the cord between you and the other person;

3. In your mind draw a circle of protection and step into it, taking it with you;

4. Tap the 9 EFT points repeating, "Release others' energies;"

5. Shower off other's energies; or

6. Strong physical exercise.

Then pay attention to the above four to see if you feel like you again.

You need to be willing to be who you are. That means learning to ground so that your life is in balance with the time you spend using your Empath abilities. You can use sex, aerobic exercise, sleep, walking outdoors, massage, stretching, sitting or standing in direct contact with the earth, looking after your pet, cleaning your home, gardening or concentrating on your paying job.

It is important to learn to pay attention to your own emotions, compared to what you pick up. This takes practice, but over time, you will learn how to separate yourself from others' emotions. Empaths are needed now more than ever in these changing times. Learn to enjoy your abilities and find balance in your life.

Characteristics of an Empath

Empaths are loving, caring, kind people who want to help others. They are often found doing volunteer work and may serve others through emotionally-demanding careers as childcare givers, medical professionals, hospice workers, midwives, and such. Most empaths came in with a mission to heal people, animals, plants, and the planet. As healers, many have taken on so much external energy that they spend most of their time trying to clear unwanted energy and recuperate from the last episode that "blew their doors off."

Here are a few characteristics of empaths who have not learned to filter out other people's emotions or manage their energy:

You constantly feel overwhelmed with emotions, and you may cry a lot, feel sad, angry, or depressed for no good reason. You may be tempted to think you are crazy for having random mood swings and bouts of unexplained fatigue. If you are a woman, it's like having PMS all the time! Unrestrained empathy can cause a person to manifest symptoms similar to bipolar (manic-depressive) disorder.

You drop by the store feeling great, but once you get in a crowd, you start feeling down, angry, sad or overwhelmed. You feel you must be coming down with something, so you decide to go home and rest.

If you've found that you can't be in public without becoming overwhelmed you may start to live the life of a hermit. But, even at home, you get depressed when you watch the news, and you cry while watching a movie. You feel horrible when a commercial for the Humane Society shows animals that need a home. You may rescue more animals than you can care for.

You feel sorry for people no matter who they are or what they have done. You feel the need to stop and help anyone in your path. You can't pass by a homeless person without giving him money-even if you don't have it to spare.

Many empaths are overweight. When they absorb stressful emotions, it can trigger panic attacks, depression as well as food, sex, and drug binges. Some may overeat to cope with emotional stress or use their body weight as a shield or buffer. In Chapter 9 of Yvonne Perry's book, she shows how to use light as protection.

Most empaths can physically and emotionally heal others by drawing the pain or ailment out of the sick person and into their bodies. For obvious reasons, this is not recommended unless you know how to keep from becoming ill in the process.

From chest pains and stomach cramps to migraines and fever, you manifest symptoms without contracting an actual illness. Later, you learn that your "ailment" coincided with the onset of a friend or family member's illness.

No one can lie to you because you can see through their facade and know what they mean. You may even know why they lied.

People-even strangers-open up and start volunteering their personal information. You may be sitting in the waiting room minding your own business and waiting for your turn when the person next to you starts sharing all kinds of personal information. You didn't ask them to, and they never considered that you might not want to hear about their drama. People may feel better after speaking with you, but you end up feeling worse because they have transferred their emotional pain to you.

Some empaths don't do well with intimate relationships. Constantly taking on their partner's pain and emotions, they may easily get their feelings hurt, desire to spend time alone rather than with the partner, feel vulnerable when having sex, and feel that they have to continually retrieve their energy when it gets jumbled with that of their partner. They may be so afraid of becoming engulfed by another person that they close up emotionally just to survive.

The ill, the suffering, and those with weak boundaries are drawn to the unconditional understanding and compassion an empath emits without even being aware of it. Until you learn how to shut out the energy of others, you may have a pretty miserable existence in which you feel like you have to be entirely alone to survive.

It's easy to see why being an empath is often very draining. No wonder that over time, some folks shut down their empathic ability. And, with that, they also shut down a vital part of their divine guidance system. Learn how to manage the amount of info-energy you receive and hear more of what is important.

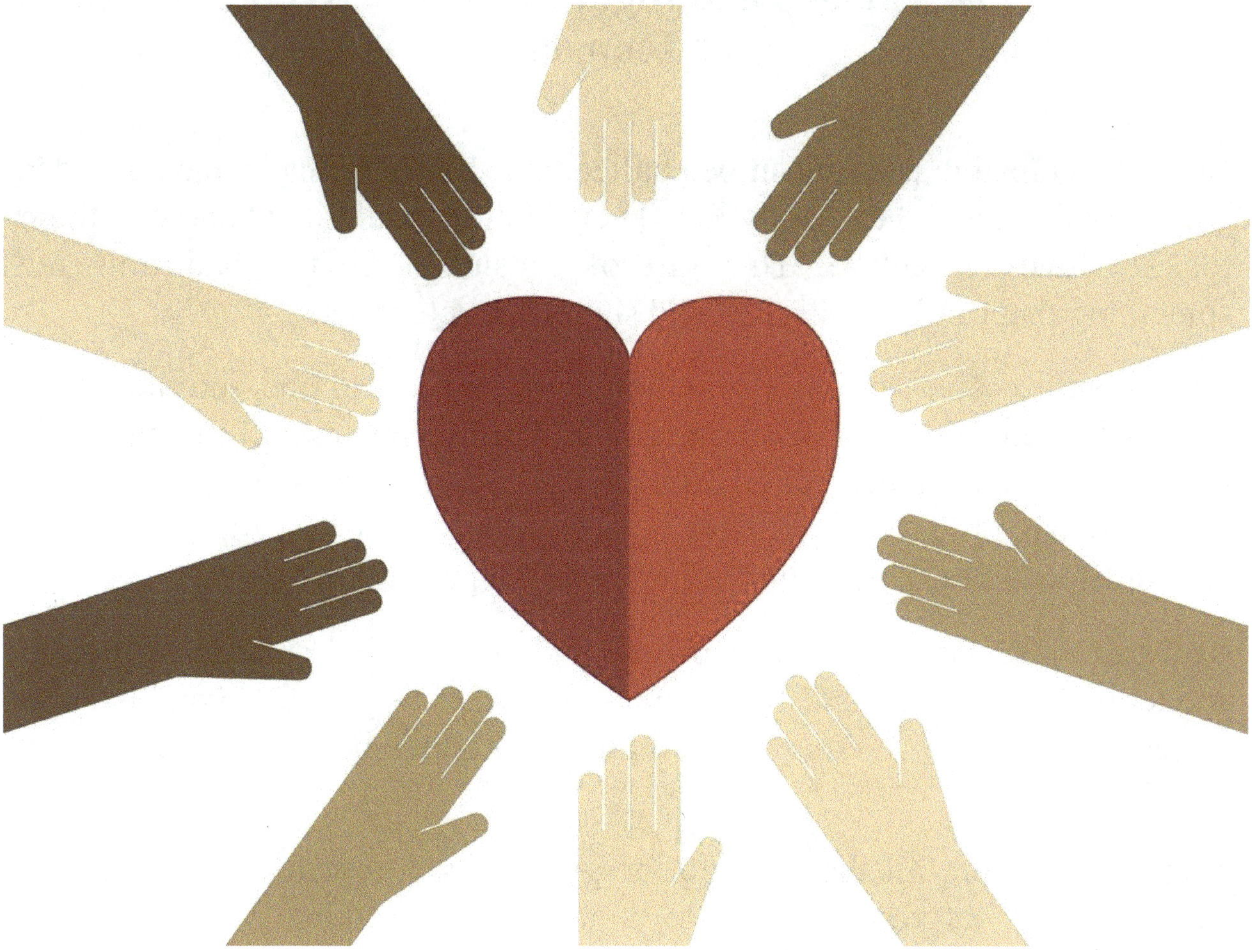

20 Things That Might Mean You Are an Empath

Being an empathic person can be challenging. Many Empaths have no idea why they feel overwhelmed by life. Their families are critical and call them too sensitive or recluse. This gift of sensitivity isn't a bad trait but something that can be controlled and should be celebrated.

An Empath receives more information about the world and activities than those who scoff at them. While it may be hard to process all the energetic information being received, an Empath can do wondrous things with this way of sensing life. Here are 20 things commonly experienced by Empaths. If your life is like this, you just might be an Empath too.

You can walk past a crowd of people and start to feel strange. You may suddenly feel angry or sad. The emotion overwhelms you, and you just have to get away. You have no explanation for your sudden changes in emotions. You just FEEL it.

You try to ignore all the rush of energy that you absorb, but you are so overwhelmed that you just want to be alone. I avoid malls for this reason and only shop at individual stores where I can dash in and back out, or I shop in open air pedestrian malls. You've been called overly sensitive all your life and usually in a negative connotation, but you know it isn't you, it's the surroundings.

You experience other physical ailments. Someone in the room has a headache, and after entering the room, you do too. You were fine before entering the room. This frequently happens to people you have relationships with, but it can occur with anyone.

You feel so lethargic that you just stay in bed. It isn't depression, but you would just rather be alone. You aren't a loner; you just need to be alone to recharge your battery. When the company leaves, you need a nap.

Your fatigue coincides with a family member's illness, but you live in another state, and there has been no communication between the two of you before your fatigue.

You experience the same symptoms as a relative's illness, but not the actual illness. For example, I was driving when my father had a stroke. I suddenly got dizzy and felt air bubbles going up through my head. I had to pull over and figure out if it was me or someone else. Later that night, I found out he had had the stroke just as I felt it.

You are overwhelmed when watching horrible thing that happen in real life or on television. Do you experience the feelings of the people involved as though you've been punched in the gut or burst into tears, shaking etc.?

You can drive over a place where there has been an accident and suddenly crumple in physical or emotional pain.

You aren't able to watch the news.

You always know what someone really means and what they meant to say.

You always know when someone is lying. I've always called this my BS Meter.

You have a knowing about situations that are more than intuition, hunches or statistical probability.

You feel compelled to care for someone even if they are unkind to you.

You feel compelled to care for someone on the spot and generally that help is accepted.

People tell you their life story and wonder why they are telling you all about it.

You can't stand In Your Face people and just want to stay away from them and generally be alone. You are very sensitive to smells, excessive talking or loud sounds. You may be so overwhelmed that you develop physical symptoms like headaches or instant colds.

You can heal instinctively by drawing pain or ailments into your own body.

You would rather drive in your car so that you can get out quickly when you start to feel overloaded.

You often feel spacey and clumsy because all the incoming energies unground you.

This list of list of possible behaviours can help you decide if you are an Empath or not. If you do feel like you are an Empath, you probably need help working with all the energy and information coming at you. Look for ways to deal with it all, and you'll find like a kinder place to be.

Empaths - The Sensitive Ones

Empaths are people whose sensitivity is much greater than that of the average Joe or Josie.

Empaths are people who:

- often get confused between their feelings and other peoples,

- can look at a person and tell what they are feeling and experiencing,

- often have difficulty being in crowded places like shopping centres or pubs,

- attract energy vampires to them (people who drain your energy) and

- can sometimes feel natural and man-made disasters before they happen,

If you are an Empath, you probably struggle with many aspects of daily life. One of the major problems with Empaths is that they tend to take on other people's emotions and issues as though they were their own. When you feel other people's feelings, you often don't realise that the emotions are coming from outside of yourself. They all tend to feel as though they are your emotions which can be very confusing and often overwhelming. After a while of accumulating emotions both yours and others, you can get very sick. To move beyond these difficulties, some new Life Skills need to be introduced and implemented.

There are some ways to counteract the problems of being an Empath. Many of them have to do with defining and clarifying who you are and what you believe. The first and most important action to take is to get focused on your thoughts and beliefs. As you come to a much clearer, more conscious awareness about who you are and what you believe compared to what others believe, you will widen the gap between yourself and other's emotions. Even if you do take on another's feelings, it will be easier to recognise them as not belonging to you. Once the recognition is made, you can easily let go of the other persons 'stuff'.

Another set of activities that is very important in clearing up the empathic difficulties is that of cleansing and protecting your energy field. There are many, many ways in which to do this, and I will offer just a few.

For cleansing the energy field, I recommend with every shower that you take; you imagine that the water is super powerful, sparkling, cleansing energy that flushes all over and through your body, easily washing away any build up of negative energy. At the same time while having the shower, in your mind, call out to Archangel Michael (the defender and protector) to come and use his powerful sword to swipe through any cords all over your body, that are draining your energy. These two activities will easily release great amounts of negative energy.

For protecting the energy, I recommend that every morning you call upon Archangel Michael and ask him to wrap his wings around you, sealing and protecting you from any negative energy throughout the day. I also suggest that using your imagination, you surround yourself with a beautiful sparkly mirrorball, that instantly reflects all negative energy away from you.

Simply by performing these four exercises daily and working on defining who you are and what you believe, you can make a real difference to your experiences in this life. After a while of doing that, you can even start to open up to the gifts of being an empath, such as having a greater level of insight into people's behaviour and their intentions. Being an Empath truly is a wonderful gift, and you can experience it as such with a bit of healing work.

CHAPTER 2

HIGHLY SENSITIVE PEOPLE

Highly Sensitive People

Just imagine what the world might be like if the highly sensitive people were in charge. Shopping malls, if they existed, would play soothing music at low volumes and eliminate the flashing lights. Restaurants would be designed such that you could talk in a normal tone and be heard by your dinner mates; shouting to be heard over the din of the other diners, the kitchen, and the wait staff a thing of the past. Television would stop emphasizing violence and focus more on the good stuff of life. Oh, those could be the days...

What is a highly sensitive person, you may be asking. I can't recall the first time I heard the term, but I do know it was shortly after the book, "The Highly Sensitive Person," by Elaine Aron, was released. It's best to read the book to get a full view, and in the spirit of

explanation I'll give a few bullet points here:

20% of the population is "wired" differently. They take in more information that the other 80%, and process it on a much deeper level. It's common for something they've experienced to stay with them twice as long as it would the others.

They may hear they are "too sensitive" from those around them, that they need tougher skin. They tend to be emotional and feel things deeply.

They notice the little things in their environment. This makes them attentive to what fabrics they wear, what type of food they eat (and how often), how well they sleep if one small thing around them changes, and what perfume the person next to them is wearing.

Why am I bringing this up? Because Leslie and I are highly sensitive people and we spent our lives up until we heard the term wondering what was wrong with us. In light of this new information we understand that there are many like us; in fact, a quick poll of those we enjoy being with shows that many of them are highly sensitive, too - who knew! Oprah always says when you know better you do better.

Applying that to this newfound knowledge about being highly sensitive, ponder these questions:

Many may feel that there is something wrong with them because of their sensitivity. Reframing this thought, how could you view your sensitivity as a good thing?

Highly sensitive people are frequently connected to others, animals and the planet on a deep level. How can this be used to make you and those around you live a better life?

What is the best way you can take care of yourself ? Perhaps it is eating more frequently, visiting spas, meeting with a group of supportive friends that share your trait, or giving yourself permission to stay in the house all day.

Learning about and living as a highly sensitive person can at once be challenging and the most rewarding thing you'll ever do. Owning our businesses, running workshops and teaching classes, developing a business alliance with a day spa, coaching one on one clients, and being part of a supportive community - our partnership first and foremost - have been terrific ways for Leslie and I to take care of our sensitivity. We encourage you to find the support you need to discover the true contribution that you are, just as you are. What first step will you take today to embrace your

Highly Sensitive People -- An Introduction to the Trait of High Sensitivity

Here is an overview and some of what I've learned during the last 9 years of intense study about the trait of high sensitivity. Also included, are some tips, tools, and strategies we've discovered on how to successfully navigate through life when you or someone important to you has the trait of high sensitivity. My goal is that I want HSPs not just to cope with their trait, but to excel with it!

I've learned highly sensitive persons or "HSPs" make up 15% to 20% of the population. (People with the trait of high sensitivity are also sometimes referred to as ultra-sensitive people, or super sensitive people.) HSP's nervous systems are different and are more sensitive to subtleties in their environment, which can be a good or bad thing. And because they process and reflect upon incoming information so deeply, they are more likely to become over stimulated and overwhelmed than Non-HSP.

Highly sensitive individuals have often said they feel they are "different" and just don't fit in; we've even heard some HSPs say they sometimes feel like they're from a different planet.

Being highly sensitive is an inherited trait and is described brilliantly in Dr Elaine Aron's book The Highly Sensitive Person: How to Thrive When the World Overwhelms You. This is a book I highly recommend.

I've also learned a great deal from Psychologist Carl G. Jung's "Psychological Types," Dr John M. Oldham's "Sensitive Personality Style," and Dr Kazimierz Dabrowski's "Theory of Positive Disintegration" and "Overexcitabilities."

It is in highly sensitive person's nature to "pause-to-check" and not to rush into new or different situations, but rather to proceed much more cautiously than their Non-HSP counterparts. The trait of high sensitivity causes them to process and reflect upon incoming information very deeply. It is not that they are "fearful" or "afraid," but that it's in their nature to process incoming information so deeply. Highly sensitive persons may even sometimes need until the next day to have had enough time to process the information fully, reflect upon it, and formulate their response.

The trait of high sensitivity can be viewed as having both positive as well as negative characteristics, and it is a valid and normal trait and is not a character flaw or disorder.

On the positive side, and there is a big positive side, we have learned highly sensitive people have wonderful imaginations, are often very intelligent, creative, curious, and are known for being very hard workers, great organizers and problem solvers. They are known for being extremely conscientious and meticulous. HSP are blessed with being exceptionally intuitive, caring, compassionate and spiritual. They are also blessed with incredible aesthetic awareness and appreciation for nature, music and the arts.

Pearl S. Buck, (1892-1973), recipient of the Pulitzer Prize in 1932 and the Nobel Prize in Literature in 1938, once said about highly sensitive people:

"The truly creative mind in any field is no more than this:

A human creature born abnormally, inhumanly sensitive.

To him...

- touch is a blow,
- a sound is a noise,
- misfortune is a tragedy,
- joy is an ecstasy,
- a friend is a lover,
- a lover is a god,
- and failure is death.

Add to this cruelly delicate organism the overpowering necessity to create, create, create - so that without the creating of music or poetry or books or buildings or something of meaning, his very breath is cut off from him. He must create, must pour out creation. By some strange, unknown, inward urgency he is not alive unless he is creating." -Pearl S. Buck

There is also a strong correlation between the trait of high sensitivity and being "Gifted." It is probably accurate to say that although not all gifted people are highly sensitive, all highly sensitive people are gifted. And, Dr Dabroski's "OE" theory is that people born with overexcitabilities have a higher level of "development potential" than others and that their overexcitabilities feed, enrich, empower and amplify their talents.

Some of the diverse group of individuals that might belong on the list of those who exhibit the characteristics of the trait of high sensitivity would include: Albert Einstein, Carl Jung, Emily Dickinson, Charles Darwin, Abraham Lincoln, Katharine Hepburn, Woody Allen, Queen Elizabeth II, Orson Welles, Walt Disney, Ansel Adams, Nicole Kidman, Nicolas Cage, Steven Spielberg, Jane Goodall, Warren Buffett, Barbara Streisand, Michael Jordan, Elton John, Bob Dylan, Jim Morrison, Jewel, John Denver, Alanis Morissette, and Princess Diana, to name a few. And, a couple of possible HSPs from TV that comes to mind include Radar O'Reilly on the classic sitcom M*A*S*H and currently Adrain Monk, the detective with OCD, on the series MONK. Some feature films portraying characters that may give some insight into the trait of high sensitivity include: "The Hours," "The Green Mile," "Amelie," "Hannibal," and "Adaptation."

We hope you'll recognise that the trait of high sensitivity is a gift and blessing, albeit a gift that can come with a hefty price tag. But, a gift we hope you'll come to realize is worth every penny of the price.

As we have come to know, the highly sensitive person's systems are very porous, that is external stimuli seems to be more directly absorbed into their bodies. (It has been said that it is as if HSP hardly have any "skin" at all to protect them from these outside stimuli.) Non-HSP is generally less porous and have natural defences which defuse external stimuli thereby not directly impacting and overloading their nervous systems.

Another way to think about this is to visualize the curve on a chart: At the point where the Non-HSP would have little or no stimulation, the HSP would be somewhat stimulated. Where Non-HSP would be somewhat stimulated, the HSP would be pretty well stimulated. And, where the Non-HSP is well stimulated, the HSP may be reaching, or might have already reached, a state of being over stimulated, over-aroused and overwhelmed, which may manifest itself in highly sensitive people as getting upset, frazzled or even angry, needing to get away, or possibly "shutting down" and becoming unable to function.

We have also learned that although many highly sensitive people are introverts, reserved, quiet or shy, there is a percentage that is high sensation seekers or extroverts. And, although they seek adventure they also get overloaded and become over stimulated with the same results as the rest of the HSP.

So, if you've ever felt you were all alone in having these overwhelming feelings and the need to seek solitude and sanctuary, we hope you find comfort in knowing that you are not alone and that you will benefit from some of the suggestions presented here.

Highly Sensitive People - Sounds, Smells and Sentiments

The first modern psychological discussion of the problems of hypersensitive and hyper-responsive people appeared in the 1930s when psychologist Carl Jung was elaborating his ideas on personality types. He speculated that approximately 25 % of his therapeutic clients were individuals who were inordinately sensitive to the stimulation coming from their surroundings. This sensitivity included, responses to sound and light and smells, as well as heightened emotional attunedness... being both easily affected by, and also very aware of, other people's feelings. He noted as well heightened attention to details of all sorts. He proposed that this sensitivity was related to a character trait which he called "introversion" and that it was also connected to the quality of "intuition".

High Sensitivity and Introversion: Introversion is no longer "low sociability."

Modern personality researchers have done hundreds of studies on the personality traits of introversion-extraversion. Early research treated it as a measure of sociability; later research looked it more generally as a physiological measure. The studies concur that introverts are:

- More physically sensitive
- More sensitive to stimuli and stimulants
- They process information more thoroughly
- They prefer to reflect before acting
- More reflective when given feedback
- More vigilant in discrimination tasks

Slower to acquire and forget information due to their deeper processing into memory

Greater sensitivity is found at all levels of the nervous system from sensitivity to pinpricks, to skin conductivity to faster reaction times

High sensitivity is innate.

You are born with it. Infant research shows that this sensitivity seems to be present from birth. Carl Jung was not far off the mark in his sense of its prevalence since current studies suggest that 15-20 % of all humans (and even animals) show the trait of high sensitivity and that it is equally divided between men and women. This non-trivial rate of appearance in the population suggests that it offered an evolutionary advantage. Individuals who are sensitive or reactive will "look before they leap" and survive to reproduce.

Hypersensitivity and PTSD

The exception to the "born with it" rule is extreme sensitivity that is associated with the after-effects of trauma.

Effects of high sensitivity on social and emotional development

Loud, busy or emotionally over-stimulating environments are harder on highly sensitive individuals. They may withdraw or minimize their exposure to these situations and develop an introverted social style.

Some highly sensitive individuals are still extroverts!

Usually, these are people who have grown up in supportive extended families where social interaction was a source of comfort, and the family "ran interference" protecting them from over-stimulation and anxiety until they had the skills to manage the world themselves. They still typically report needing a lot of "down time" to recuperate after social encounters.

Negative family environments

Highly sensitive children born into less supportive families who do not recognize their special vulnerability and protect them often grow up to be anxious, withdrawn or emotionally avoidant.

- Highly sensitive people are highly sensitive to their internal bodily processes too.

- Chronic over-arousal is a common source of stress for sensitive individuals.

Highly sensitive people often present medically with stress-related illnesses and environmental sensitivities.

These illnesses may sometimes be dismissed by others as "psychosomatic" especially since their less sensitive fellows would not be so easily overwhelmed.

Psychosomatic symptoms may indeed be produced as the individual unconsciously seeks socially acceptable ways to reduce their activity and over-stimulation.

Highly sensitive people are often accused of indecisiveness and slow decision making.

Their deep and detailed processing of information and ideas takes longer than other peoples.

Human empathy is based on our ability to read subtle emotional signals.

Individuals who are more sensitive and more vigilant naturally become better readers of these signals. Some sensitive persons have problems in intimate relationships since:

They respond so strongly to criticism.

Their detailed consideration of all aspects of life makes them prone to spot flaws in others and become irritated by their loved one's minor annoying habits.

They try to control and tune their environment to a level that they find tolerable.

With prevalence in the population of 15 to 20% that makes almost one in five of our friends and relatives "highly sensitive."

High sensitivity then is both a blessing and a curse and a normal part of the colourful spectrum of human character.

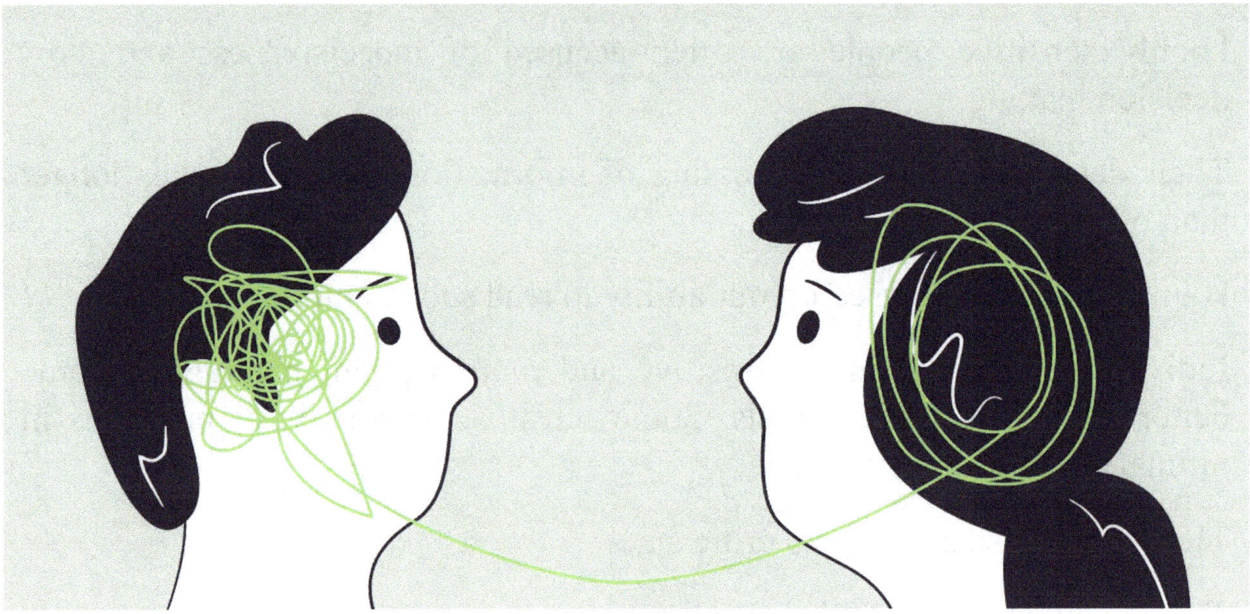

Highly Sensitive People Traits and Characteristics

Being highly sensitive is just one variety of the different personalities all of us possess. Highly sensitive people have been branded as the ones who react in a very expressive way than most people do. They can be intimidated by the slightest stimuli they receive, may it be from a beeping clock to a talkative coworker. But these people are not basing their actions solely on their emotions; on the contrary, they are very intellectual and tend to analyze things better than the others. They have negative and positive traits which can be used to their advantage or disadvantage.

Let us try to understand the various traits and characteristics of highly sensitive people by exploring every aspect of their lives. Emotionally, these people are often seen as shy or socially inhibited. They are not commonly seen interacting with people in hallways or chatting in restrooms. Most of them are introverted and like keeping to themselves. Since they were young, they have learned not to show awareness of other people's emotions.

If you are going to observe an HSP physically, you will note that most of them do not like being exposed to glaring light or in places with loud noises. Even strong odours are unappealing to these people. They think more of themselves and how they feel, and they know when they do not belong to an environment.

The introverted HSP's often feel like they do not belong in social gatherings, they are satisfied with their own company and are very much comfortable when left alone. After being forced to interact with people, they usually take time off to cool down and relax, as if relating to others is a very stressful situation.

The psychological characteristic of HSPs is extreme protectiveness of themselves and their personal spaces. Even their workspace does not allow intruders. There are also some who are trying to hide this protective nature by being all out, showing the opposite. After which, they get stressed too much which results in overstimulation even anxiety.

In terms of personal relationships, they tend to be difficult to handle. Personal issues often get in their way of relating to their partners. But the best thing that they can offer their partners is their intuitive thought and deep analogies.

Work and career is the most challenging aspect in the lives of HSP's. This is because most workplaces require you to relate with other people to do your work. But since HSP's are very creative, they have found many jobs where they feel comfortable such as one-on-one jobs and doing solo work. They are the best writers, programmers, web designers and excel on tasks which are handled alone.

In the cultural aspect, HSP's are not into the outgoing ideals of modern trends. But most of them can tolerate the changes in culture as long as they are not forced to portray such expressions.

Family problems tend to overwhelm HSP's. If they had a bad childhood, chances are they go on with their lives in denial because they find it difficult to forget situations where their emotions are challenged. But since they practice being tough, these scars do not show on their faces.

Spiritually, HSP's are blessed to be far more intuitive; they are into deep soul searching in search for the inner warmth. In their quiet times, they always find time to connect with the Supreme Being.

One in every twenty people is considered to be a highly sensitive person (HSP). This means that either you may be sensitive or someone you know is. 42% of the population is not highly sensitive, meaning that most things don't bother them the way they will an HSP. Everyone else falls somewhere in between, with the odd few being completely unemotional about anything. (By the way - 20% of the entire animal kingdom is highly-sensitive as well).

Who are HSP's and What Are They Like?

We're the thinkers, the cautious ones, the conservative people; the ones that say "Hey, wait a minute. Let's think this through before doing something rash."

Every society needs highly sensitive people, just as we need the warriors, the leaders who are ready to take risks. However, we're the ones that help to temper the not-so-sensitive types, the ones who can be bold, rash and impulsive and may not have thought things through to the consequences of their actions. Highly sensitive people are most often the people found in the roles of advisors, counsellors and advocators for restraint.

Unfortunately, in western society, we've also been labelled as somewhat "defective", according to the way non-HSP's see us. We're considered "too sensitive, too cautious, too shy, too timid, too introverted, too fearful." What needs to be realized is that these are not "problems" that need to be corrected and fixed with sensitive people. It's the labels that are attached to us that cause the problems. Many non-sensitive people are also shy, timid, introverted and fearful, while there are many highly sensitive people who are out-going, super-friendly, extroverted, and risk-takers. We just tend to think things through first and weigh all the factors that our senses pick up on before forging ahead.

Traits and Characteristics Misinterpreted

So, what are some of the traits and characteristics of a highly sensitive person? Let's look at some of the facts and the mythical labels that have been attached to this special group.

Shyness

- You'll probably find a larger portion of shy people in the HSP group. That does not mean that everyone is shy. That's a myth. A lot of non-sensitive people are also shy. Sometimes, what's mistaken as shyness is a sizing up of the situation and the people that we have just met. We're cautious. If our senses are saying something isn't right about the person, we won't be so open to them. First impressions count. It's not just the way the person is dressed, but their whole demeanour, aura, attitude and other little subtleties that we absorb with all of our senses. We process the thoughts, feelings and sensations that we receive in each new situation. This may make some of us appear "shy", when we're not.

Introverted

- Somewhat of a myth. You'll find many HSP's can be extroverted, outgoing and fun-loving. You'll also find many non-sensitive people as being introverted. Don't mistake deep-thinking and inner-reflection as introversion. We do require much more alone time. This is because our nervous systems can go into overload in a situation that a non-sensitive person would find somewhat stimulating. If we become frazzled and over-stimulated, we need to find a quiet spot as soon as possible to settle back down. This is why many HSP's tend to stay at home more often than not, rather than go out to party. It's not that we don't want to... we just know our systems can't handle the overload for too long a time. If we can't get away, we'll pull into ourselves, as a sort of protective shield, to try to reduce the noise, sights, sounds and smells that are bombarding us to calm down.

Fearfulness

Unless you're completely unemotional and have a lack of conscious consideration toward others, who can say that they've never been fearful at times? This is not an exclusive trait of sensitive people. New experiences often cause butterflies, fearful thoughts and inner-turmoil in most people. HSP's just tend to feel those emotions more deeply.

Timidness

- Caution, careful evaluation of the situation, needing the see the "entire picture", and the possible resulting consequences of our actions is just in our nature. If everyone heedlessly rushed into everything, we'd have even more chaos in our world than we do now.

Too-Sensitive

Yes, this is our major trait. We assimilate everything around us at once. Lights, noises, smells, energy vibrations, they all get absorbed, processed and evaluated. Unfortunately, when there are too much activity and noise around us, we can't handle it for a great length of time. For example, what may be low to moderate level of music for a non-sensitive person could sound like the level of a rock concert to us. Emotionally, we're affected by much of the disharmony in the world. We feel another person's heartache; we are aware of low levels of anger or resentment in a room, we empathize with other people's problems, and feel great sorrow over horrific tragedies.

What Does All This Mean?

A highly sensitive person will pick up on subtleties in the surroundings that many non-sensitive people can't see or feel. This can give us some great advantages. It can save us in many situations where there's trouble brewing. Our abilities can keep us from making disastrous business or personal decisions if we follow our instincts. And because of our deep sense of the environment around us, we're often the ones that make others aware of potential environmental problems that unscrupulous companies ignore for their benefits. HSP's are often the ones that push for reforms and changes in government law for the better good of everyone.

As with anything, it's good to know that you're not alone, that there are others out there that have to deal with the same types of situations and "labels" as you do. True, it doesn't hurt any less, but you know there are similar types that you can seek out and talk to...and they'll understand. Yes, we do tend to exhibit more of the above traits and characteristics than non-sensitive people do, but we're not exclusive owners of them either. Sometimes, it's a misinterpretation of what's going on in the mind of an HSP by non-HSP's. Only another highly sensitive person could understand. The good news is that highly sensitive people have been around for as long as man has walked the earth and we'll always be here, working to make the world a more understanding, considerate and peaceful haven for everyone.

Ten Ways to Tell If You Are an Extra Sensitive Person

It wasn't until I was back in the quiet of my own house that I felt the drain of energy. I had been at a very pleasant party and didn't exert any "out of the ordinary" energy. But as soon as I returned to my environment, I felt it. I was exhausted, tired beyond measure, like I could go to bed and sleep for a week. And it was only 9:00 p.m.! It was in that moment I finally accepted that I am one of those extra sensitive people (ESP) that I so often work within my practice. If you have ever felt the type of energy drain that I did, simply from being in a crowded room, you too may be an extra sensitive person. Here are some other clues that your sensitivity may be getting the best of you.

- You go through phases of crying or being defensive at the drop of a hat.

- You experience unexplained mood swings, especially after being around others.

- Your friends tell you, or you know yourself, that you're very intuitive.

- You will often lose yourself in a good book, tv, video game or some other solitary behaviour.

- You insulate yourself from your feelings with food, alcohol or any of the above behaviours.

- You are easily overwhelmed when you are presented with a lot of information at once.

- You have unexplained aches and pains or health issues.

- You are most comfortable in serene, soothing surroundings. Loud or harsh environments are like poison to you.

- You get overwhelmed when thinking about the pain and suffering in the world.

- You will often pick up on the needs of others and help them before they even ask.

There are many gifts which come with being an ESP, such as the ability to help others and heightened intuition. Unfortunately, your sensitivity may be getting in the way of realizing them. If you saw yourself on this list, it is most important for you to first accept your sensitivity and then take healthy measures to take care of yourself. Start with the basics, plenty of rest, hydration, healthy food, and exercise to ground you. Self-reflection is a must, and a good self-care plan will help you get a handle on your extra sensitivity. Extra sensitivity (ESP), when you managed it effectively, can be thoroughly enjoyed.

The Emotional Rollercoaster of Empaths and Highly Sensitive People

There is much more information on the traits of Highly Sensitive People (HSP's) which I won't go into here. If you are one, you know it!

I haven't, however, been able to find much information on one particular trait of HSP's, the ability to sense and feel other peoples' emotions. This empathic ability alone can have a devastating effect on the way that the HSP experiences the world.

To experience feelings that aren't your own can cause havoc, especially when it is not understood. This is not just a logical thought process or something that you 'think' is happening to someone but a 'taking on board' of that emotion ourselves. To the point that we feel it, live it out and process it just as though it were our own.

When emotions are occurring within ourselves without an apparent cause it generates confusion, upset and a gradual lowering of self-esteem. If there are no reasons for this constant emotional rollercoaster, then we can only assume that we are emotionally unstable, feeling things that we don't understand and with no apparent way out of it. This is particularly true of the negative emotions that can tend to stick like glue.

Suddenly finding yourself depressed, angry or irritable when you were feeling perfectly OK a few minutes before can become so normal that it becomes a way of life. A constant sense of 'not feeling right' within, anxious, tense and on edge can be a sign that you are living in an energy that is not yours, almost like wearing someone else's clothes that just don't fit.

I believe that we are all unconsciously affected by other people's energies. Being empathic, however, with this depth of feeling in everyday life takes it to a new level. Being called 'moody', 'too sensitive', 'emotionally unstable' or worse 'mad' does little to help an already confused state as to why you feel as much as you do.

So every person that you come into contact with, everyone that you think of (or who is thinking about you) can affect your energy and how you are feeling. Deep joy? Not! This can be an extremely difficult thing to live with when there is no understanding of what is occurring.

The majority of people do not experience this level of empathy and are therefore not going to understand it. Because it is not considered normal or widely understood, it can cause further confusion and constant questioning of 'what's wrong with me?'

The most traumatic part of this experience, for me, is that you are unlikely to ever get confirmation from others that it is their emotion and not yours. Even when you are with someone who understands this ability, they may not be aware of their depths of emotion and the constant shifts that occur. Sometimes people do not know themselves at this level and the emotion they experience, they are unaware of the thoughts and beliefs they carry and the subsequent emotional reactions.

It is empathic means that you feel the emotion from others even when they are unaware of it themselves. It means that you feel subtle shifts that are not perceivable to anyone else. It is not only strong emotional energies that are sensed; it could be a fleeting sense of irritation, fear, nervousness or any other emotion.

I spent many years trying to get confirmation from other people that it wasn't my emotion that I was experiencing. This doesn't work! To be met with a general response of 'no, it's not me' confuses you even more as others can be adamant they are not feeling something, they are genuinely unaware of it.

So what can you do about this? It takes time to realise that all you are experiencing may not be yours, to consider that you may be empathic. Its useful to start being very aware of your emotional state, to notice when you are at ease and when you are not. To note how you feel before you are with other people and then to note any changes that occur.

This is difficult at first when you have spent a lifetime just accepting the emotional shifts as normal. Difficult because you can find yourself in the throes of an emotional reaction without even being aware of it starting, or of where it came from.

It is a case of getting to know yourself, your emotional reactions and thought processes so that then, you know without a doubt that you are experiencing something that is not your own. You find a place where you have your 'normal' and anything outside of that might not be yours.

Our thoughts will create emotional shifts in ourselves, as they do with everyone, but you can generally be aware of your own 'stuff' that can cause emotional reactions.

I have come to realise that the vague sense of unease I often experience comes from not being in my energy and from living in someone else's. This means that I am taking away that persons experience and processing something that doesn't belong to me.

Understanding Highly Sensitive People

Sometimes they are called wimps, shy, nerds, neurotics, and at other times, like in the ancient past, they were known as intuitives, sages, and wise people.

Who are these interesting people?

They are the 20 per cent of the population that psychologist Dr Elaine Aron PhD calls Highly Sensitive People (HSP). Dr Aron, a self-described Highly Sensitive Person, has written several books that explain the sensitivity phenomenon and offer helpful tips for living a healthy life, fully, and happily as a sensitive person. She has helped many to understand that:

* Sensitive people are more aware of the subtleties in other people, places and things in their environment and therefore observe, reflect upon and experience more than non-sensitive people.

* Sensitivity is related to a survival strategy that inspires humans and other creatures to observe and assess situations before they proceed into them.

* The brains of sensitive beings are more active and work differently than non-sensitives.

* Different cultures value or devalue sensitivity in different ways. Low self-esteem issues are common among sensitive people because of this.

* Sensitivity is still misunderstood and was once thought to be a disorder to be treated.

With 20 per cent of the population being sensitive you probably know at least one sensitive or maybe even live with one. Perhaps it is time to consider these people in a new light and value them for the gifts that they bring into our lives. Highly Sensitive People tend to be very intelligent, conscientious and pay attention to the smallest details, so they make great employees. Because they are intuitive to other people's needs, they make great counsellors, massage therapists, coaches and tutors. Their observance of details and nuances in their environment make them ideal visual artists and musicians, and if you want someone to guide you with money management, choose an HSP because they are usually three steps ahead of the stock market and your personal needs.

Living with acute sensitivity can be a gift as it leads to great personal awareness, compassion for others and the development of skills that can assist others. The challenges of living with your sensory skills constantly registering information can be devastating if one does not realize that they are sensitive. Before developing awareness and management skills for their sensitivity, many HSP work extra hard at trying to be "normal".

They will accompany their family or friends into settings that they find uncomfortable (loud, cluttered, crowded, overstimulating), and endure a horrible experience, to avoid loneliness or just to be like the others. Many HSP tries to keep the pace of non-sensitive people and end up experiencing burn out. Because they experience so much more sensory experience, HSP needs more sleep and downtime than other people.

It is almost like they live three days condensed into a single day. Mental health days are a priority for HSP. Unfortunately, many adults are unaware that they are HSP, and they try to live their lives like the other 80 per cent and begin self-medicating with alcohol or drugs just to get through a day.

My theory is that most people with serious addiction issues are HSP and they use their drug of choice to muffle their sensory reception.

As children, many HSP is labelled as shy, fussy, inhibited, fearful, or challenged in some way. If we could change places with that child for a few minutes, we would realize that they are indeed wise, thoughtful, creative, intuitive and quite caring for others. Unfortunately, these children are easily overwhelmed, especially in a school setting where noise, visual stimulation, and topic shuffling are normal (a Feng Shui nightmare if you ask me!), and they sometimes express their discomfort through uncooperative behaviour.

Instead of implementing behaviour management techniques that are designed for the other 80 per cent of the population perhaps the offering of a quieter space, the ability to leave the classroom for sensory breaks and adopting a better understanding of their experience by teachers and caregivers could be considered. Instead of sending your child to their room as punishment, suggest that they go to their special space for some relaxing or creative time.

When you empower a Highly Sensitive Child to learn how to care for themselves at an early age, you are giving them a gift of self-respect and self-acceptance that may remain with them throughout their life. This can help them to create healthy and fulfilling lives as adults and avoid a life of suffering like many unaware HSP.

5 Myths about Highly Sensitive People

A highly sensitive person is someone who tends to be attuned to their surroundings. They are often intuitive and empathic, have a keen imagination and may feel very overwhelmed by noise, chaos and crowds. They can have trouble fitting in and have been perceived as "too shy" or "too sensitive."

Many people object to the term 'highly sensitive' because it is often thought of as being a bad thing. Some prefer terms like highly attuned or highly aware since those terms don't carry the negative connotation of being 'overly sensitive.'

It can be difficult to understand or relate to highly sensitive people. I think that's mostly because we don't understand ourselves. I certainly didn't for most of my life. Because we were seen as being different from everyone else when we were growing up, other people, particularly our parents and family, didn't know how to relate to us. A highly sensitive person often tries very hard to fit in but is unable to do so, and so they conclude that there must be something wrong with them. We're often told things like "you're too sensitive;" "get over it;" "you're childish, grow up;" and, my personal favourite "don't be so stupid." As if when we say that we are uncomfortable in certain situations or don't want to do certain things, we're just difficult.

If you are highly sensitive or know someone who is, these tips might help you have a better understanding of what it means:

We're not delicate. Being sensitive simply means that we are more tuned in to the environment and the people around us. We pick up on things that most others do not. We notice things. It doesn't mean that we will fall apart if you are direct and honest with us (in fact we prefer it because then we know where we stand with you).

There's nothing wrong with us. We are not broken. We do not need fixing. We are just different. We don't often enjoy the same things that many others enjoy - and this isn't just in our heads, it's a physical thing. We feel physical symptoms that are uncomfortable in response to things like noise, fluorescent lighting, smoke, perfumes, chemical smells, crowds, chaotic environments, and so on.

We are not unsociable, nor do we think that we're better than everyone else. Those who are highly sensitive and also introverts can respond to over-stimulation by withdrawing and becoming quiet. We may decline to join you at a bar or an event where there are lots of people, not because we're unsociable, but because we know we wouldn't enjoy it, and we would suffer afterwards. We know, from experience, that it can take us days to recover from such over-stimulation.

Not all highly sensitive people are introverts and vice versa. There are people who are extroverted and yet also highly sensitive. The difference is that an introverted HSP will tend to withdraw when experiencing over-stimulation, while an extrovert may lash out and become aggressive or angry. Although again, this depends on the person, not all extroverted HSP's will act this way.

It's easy to think that HSP's might not thrive in leadership positions. The opposite is true. They can thrive (although they may not always want to). HSP's make great leaders because they can be more in-tune with the other members of their team and have a wider perspective. They also tend to pick up on things that others might miss - such as emotions, body language, facial expressions - because they are so highly aware.

There's no doubt about it, being highly sensitive can be difficult. But those difficulties are greatly reduced, and your sensitivities can be turned into great strengths once you fully understand and own who you are. It's easy to think there must be something wrong with you when you are not the same as the majority of other people. But being different is not a problem, it's a gift. Learn who you are and when challenging situations come up, help others to understand. Don't expect them to automatically know; you must help them - and know how to help yourself

CHAPTER 3

EMPHATIC ABILITIES

Empathic Psychic Abilities - Do You Possess This Type of Psychic Ability?

An empath or empathic person refers to someone that can sense or feel another's emotions. Empaths, are also known as highly sensitive people or sensitives and have the natural ability to connect with another's true emotions and can relate to a person on a much deeper level than the emotions the persona is displaying. Empaths experience empathy as is to family, friends, co-workers, pets, nature and inanimate objects. The gift of empathy is not restricted to time or space. Therefore, an empathic person can feel the emotions of people from a distance.

My Wife's Empathic Experience

As a young girl, I remember getting feelings about things. Back then,

I was completely convinced that I struggled with anxiety issues or some other form of mental health issue. I would have physical reactions of panic or stress on days when I was having a perfectly good day, and my thoughts were unrelated to emotions I was feeling. I have always been easily tearful when watching sad movies, and seeing or hearing someone going through difficult times is hard for me to be around without being emotional. At one point, I was so stressed by all of this "anxiety" that I saw several doctors and was successful with obtaining perceptions for anxiety medication only to realize that it did nothing for the emotions I was experiencing. Over time, I came to connect with this "issue" as I referred to it and realized I could predict things based on how I felt. It was less confusing to me when I could attach the feeling to a particular person. Once that happened, I was able to convince myself that it was normal because I mostly connected these feelings to my family and my closest friends. I rationalized that it must be an extension of our closeness or love by being able to feel what they were feeling. As ridiculous as that may seem to some, I was even forced to throw out that theory after a strange experience while in college.

It was my last class of the day in a packed auditorium with a lecture on finance on the menu. The auditorium was completely silent while students listened to the instructor and took notes. I was taking notes as well and suddenly began to feel so uncomfortable. I became restless and nervous. I shrugged it off and then felt as if someone had put a pillow over my face. The realization hit me, I was having one of my "anxiety attacks", and I didn't want to have it in the middle of my class. Feeling completely embarrassed that I was going to have to disturb the lecture, I began to squeeze off out my desk and grab my belongings, I took a deep breath and just got up and left. Immediately upon exiting the auditorium, I saw a close friend waiting outside for me. She was visibly upset and all at once the feelings of anxiety I had subsided. After she calmed down a bit, she told me that she had just left the apartment of a friend of the guy she was dating. While waiting on her boyfriend to arrive, his friend attacked her, put a pillow over her face, and attempted to sexually assault her. I didn't know if I was more shocked to hear the story or the fact that I was sitting through the class experiencing the emotions of what she was going through. From that day, I began to accept that for whatever reason, I had this "issue", and I wasn't as bothered by it.

It wouldn't be until many years later and frequent experiences of dealing with my "issue," that I reached out to a psychic for relationship questions. The first thing she said was that " you know you are very psychic" and at that moment, I answered her "yes." I didn't quite resonate with her style of reading, so I connected with another empathic psychic medium about a week later from my hometown, again for relationship issues. Very early in this reading, this psychic said, " You know you are very empathic." That along with her style, accuracy, and personality kept me coming back for readings, and she finally talked me into helping me develop my gift. The biggest lessons I learned during my psychic development was that it was no reason to fear the gift of empathy, and also that this gift was a huge part of my life purpose-rescue. Not to mention, I was finally able to stop calling it my "issue" and embrace it as a gift that is to be utilized in the service of others. Acknowledging and accepting my gift has allowed me to help people and has helped me to feel more connected to my spirituality.

Empathic Traits

Empathic traits and characteristics will vary with each. As with any metaphysical gift, no two people or two psychics will interpret messages the same way or sense and feel them the same way. The gift of empathy never comes alone; it is always accompanied by other metaphysical gifts and with creative gifts such as art, writing, or music. Empaths tend to express high levels of creativity and are full of imagination. Best described as great listeners or listeners of life. Empaths are natural healers and are often here on the life theme of rescue. They often find themselves helping others while putting aside their personal needs and desires. Empathic people are often great problem solvers and great thinkers. Most empaths do not discover that they are empathic until later in life.

The unique thing I have found about being empathic is the knowledge that I chose to bring this gift with me to be a part of my physical experience. It is this very knowledge that has allowed me to accept this gift and ignore the scrutiny of people that do not understand this gift or refuse to accept it as a part of their experience. Releasing my fears and being more aware of how to best use my gift is serving me well and has allowed me to truly embrace myself.

Empathic Psychic Abilities - Psychic Guide

What are Empathic Psychic Abilities?

An empathic psychic is also known as an "empath". Empaths can sense and experience the feelings of others, similar to the way telepaths can sense the thoughts of others. Empathy and telepathy are closely related to psychic abilities.

Usually, clairsentient psychics, (psychics with "clear feeling"), possess empathic psychic abilities. Empathic abilities are rare, but not unheard of.

Characteristics of an Empath

Empaths display these characteristics:

- Extreme sensitivity to the feelings of others
- An acute awareness of their surroundings
- Clear understanding of body language
- Strong knowledge of human emotion
- The ability to feel deeper than others
- The Empathic Spectrum

Not all psychics have the same amount of empathic power. Some psychics have only basic empathic abilities, while others have extremely advanced empathic powers. Most empaths fall somewhere in the middle.

Psychics with the most basic empathic abilities can sense what another is feeling, and can sometimes feel their emotions. These psychics can only understand some of what others are feeling.

Psychics with the most advanced empathic abilities can feel everything that other's are feeling. When engaged in empathic practice, these psychics often become so engaged people's feelings, that they momentarily lose sight of their own identity. Psychics such as these may be able to send emotional signals and project their feelings onto others.

Empathic Healing

Many empaths choose to use their abilities to heal others. Empaths usually place their hands on someone, to understand what they are feeling. This way, an empath can focus directly on what the patient needs.

Powerful empathic psychics can share the feelings of others, to relieve their pain. Loss and grief are two common feelings that a powerful empath can share and lessen. To reverse this method, a psychic can also share their feelings to spread joy and happiness.

A Gift or a Curse?

Because empaths spend so much time worrying about the feelings of others, they can forget to worry about themselves. Empaths may experience poor health as a result of self-neglect, emotional stress, and physical fatigue.

On the other hand, healing and spreading feelings of joy is a rare and wonderful gift!

Hopefully, you've learned something about empaths and empathic psychic abilities.

What does this mean?

If you think you might have empathic psychic abilities, you must develop your skills to uncover your true psychic power. Otherwise, your empathic power will never amount to anything useful! What a waste!

It is sometimes hard to tell whether or not someone is an empath, (a psychic who possesses empathic abilities). The problem is, you don't always know if someone possesses these psychic powers, or if they are just sensitive, understanding people. How do you know if you're empathic?

Empaths are extremely sensitive to the feelings of those around them. Often, an empath will be able to sense what someone is experiencing, even if they can't see or hear that person. Someone with this kind of ability simply "knows." Many psychics with empathic abilities report experiencing someone else's feelings as though they were their own, though this is not always the case.

A psychic with this kind of ability will be able to sense the feelings of others, especially if those feelings are very strong. Common feelings that an empath will experience include fear, joy, loneliness, excitement, love, and foreboding. The stronger the feeling, the easier it will be for the empath to sense, understand, and feel.

The thing that sets empaths apart from other, "normal" people, is that they have a deeper, more sensitive understanding of what they are feeling. This intuition comes from within and is far greater than what most people experience. For example, a "normal" person might realize that someone they love is upset by little things they say or do. However, an empath would sense this even without seeing or talking to that person, and an empath could sense if that loved one was feeling betrayed, jealous, angry, or hurt. This psychic intuition would come from within, not from the visual or audible clues of the physical world.

Empaths can tell when something is wrong, even if that something hasn't happened yet. They are overcome with a deep sense of foreboding that warns them that everything is not as it should be. A "normal" person, on the other hand, would not be able to tell when something unexpected or dangerous was going to happen.

These things all sound great, but not everyone realizes that it can also be very difficult to be an empath. This is because empaths are not able to "shut off" their abilities whenever they want. That is, they cannot choose whether or not to feel something. Instead, they must feel whatever their psychic intuition senses, even if they would rather not. This is a huge burden for empaths, and it is also why empathic psychics can get sick from exhaustion.

Although many people have heard of empaths, (psychics who can sense or feel the emotions of others), few people fully understand what it means to possess empathic psychic abilities. People naively assume that this ability is a great and wonderful gift and that it does not come at a cost to the psychic who possesses it. The truth is, this rare talent can also be a deadly burden to bear.

These psychics come wide ranges of sensitivity. On one end of the spectrum are the empathic psychics who can only vaguely recognize other people's feelings, while on the other end there are the powerful psychics who feel people's emotions as though they were their own.

Admittedly, it can be wonderful to be able to understand another person's feelings, and to be able to understand them and to help them cope with their feelings if they need help; empathic psychics are often skilled at emotional healing therapy. This is a process in which the psychic can share the burden of extreme emotion, thereby lessening the pain that it is causing the patient. Alternatively, a psychic can guide a patient through difficult emotional distress by using their sensitive, intimate understanding of a patient's emotional state of mind.

However, people don't realize that an empathic psychic doesn't necessarily choose whether or not to experience another person's feelings. Instead, they simply must accept the feelings that come to them. They constantly suffer invasions of their emotional self. They may become confused as to which feelings are their own, and which feelings come from outside sources.

What's worse, an empath usually senses extreme emotions before they experience subtle emotions. As a result, psychics must share the feelings of people in extreme emotional states, rather than the feelings of people in normal emotional states of mind. For an empathic psychic, even something as simple as walking down the street, or going to the grocery store, can be extremely emotionally taxing.

Think about it-having to constantly feel the emotions of others all the time, and without choosing to can have crippling effects on someone's psyche. Often, empathic psychics "lose themselves" in the feelings of others, and this can lead to self-doubt, confusion, loneliness, and depression.

Psychics who see their ability more as a burden than as a gift should find help by counselling with other empathic psychics who are in similar situations. Having a support network can make a living with this ability much more bearable, and can significantly improve a psychic's quality of life.

Yes, empaths possess a rare, wonderful gift that has the power to heal and help others, but it comes at an enormous cost. Is it worth it?

Empathic Abilities - What Are They and How to Tell If You Have Them

Empaths are rather intuitive beings, more adept at reading people than "signs" or tarot cards. There are people of an empathic nature that have those abilities, but that is just a small part of what is an Empath.

Interest in the empathic person has only emerged in recent times following the work of Jad Alexander. A student of psychology, Jad began to recognize certain types of people that had unique and elevated levels of sensitivity. They were very intuitive, being able to sense things at a level unknown and unavailable to the average person. He came to the conclusion after 30 years of studying such types, that they were in fact gifted, possessing the ability to "know" things intuitively such as; when someone wanted them to call, when someone was in trouble and needed help, or even how to get somewhere without ever having been there or following directions.

He concluded that these people had unique alterations to their central nervous systems (CNS). The interaction between the CNS and the brain was unique to the point that it created a "sixth sense", one that received messages at a much deeper level than "ordinary" individuals, and processed all those messages in an unconventional way. Those this phenomenon has not yet been evaluated by science, many individuals have invested time and resources into investigating exactly what is an Empath.

Through these studies, it has been determined that those with empathic natures posses particular common qualities. The most common denominator is a heightened sense of sensitivity. Often these people are labelled as over-sensitive individuals, but perhaps ultra-sensitive is a more appropriate definition. They are extremely receptive to smells, noise, and light, their sensory organs having a low threshold which amplifies the degree to which their senses react.

In addition to these heightened levels of sensitivity, Empaths are often bombarded with a constant flow of random, seemingly irrational thoughts and emotions. This is because they often "pick up" the thoughts and feelings of others, not just those in their immediate vicinity, but often of people who are miles, if not oceans away. This is the psychic make-up of what is an Empath, a condition that those unaware of their gift struggle with. Because of the huge amounts of information they are receiving, and not understanding its nature, many become overwhelmed and confused, often seeking psychological counselling, or even medication.

You may wonder, What is an Empath as opposed to a psychic . The simple explanation is; while a psychic "sees," an empathic person "feels." The hunches and gut-feelings the empathic personality experiences are psychic messages. The problem is that these messages are communicated in a type of psychic language that is both foreign and complex. Understanding this language, known as Dreamtongue, is critical to fully grasping exactly what is an Empath.

Becoming the Ultimate Empathizer

Empathy is the ability to identify with and the vicarious experiencing the feelings, thoughts, or attitudes of another person. Empathy is the capacity to understand and respond to the other's experiences.

Can you see any advantage of that in terms of persuasion? I sure can. I've been using it as a secret weapon for years in my persuasion, and I'll now share it with you.

Here's an exercise to help you get into the affluent mindset of your clients...

It's all about understanding and responding to their experiences. You may have heard of another powerful technique like this where you metaphorically 'jump' into them. Here, we are instead going to experience them.

When someone feels that kind of trust - where you are experiencing what they are going through - rapport is never far behind.

With loved ones whose patterns we know and understand, this comes naturally. This exercise you will give you an insight into people you don't know that well (if at all).

For this exercise, you'll need a partner. Here's the set up:

Ask your partner to think of anything. Call it 'A'. Notice how their body is arranged - facial features, breathing, muscle tension, gestures, etc. - and take a mental snapshot. This is how they represent thought 'A'.

Next, have them break state by looking around the room and naming three things they see. (This is just to get their mind off of 'A' and to revert to their normal state.)

Now, have them think of something qualitatively different, though not necessarily opposite. Call it 'B'.

[NOTE: When you first do this exercise thinking of the opposite may make it easier, but I encourage you to develop your skills and not use something opposite once you've got the hang of it.]

Okay, now have them break state again.

Next, have them think about either the A or B thought, without telling you which. Your job is to tell which one they're thinking about, just by looking at them. Which snapshot do they resemble the most?

Once you've done this enough times, switch roles and let them enjoy the experience of being able to tell what you're thinking. You can begin to know the people you deal with regularly.

Now you don't practice this with your prospects. You're not going to sit down with them and say, "okay, now let's practice a persuasion technique..." You practice this with the people you know well so that you can fine-tune your observation skills.

After a while, you will begin to recognize the smallest state changes in others as you converse with them. When they speak about certain topics, give you certain answers, you will experience them, and they will feel it too.

Although they will not be able to pinpoint the feeling they get, they will feel connected to you.

So what's the value in this? Certainly, it's a fast and effective way to gain rapport. It also puts the person in a state of feeling understood.

Another way this can be valuable is in determining whether or not a client is lying. Not that you need to interrogate a client, but knowing if someone's fibbing is always useful.

If a prospect, for instance, explains that their finances are "great" but their body language belies this, then these verbal and nonverbal cues can be a dead give away that this prospect doesn't have a steady hold on his finances - and this information can be used to your persuasive advantage.

You can use other persuasive strategies to get this prospect to open up about their financial situation. And once you do that, you gain even more rapport, you get to the heart of their problem, and you can immediately introduce yourself and your service as the solution to their problem.

How to Empathize with Your Partner Better

We might not be aware of it, but we are an extremely narcissistic society. This is becoming a problem that could undermine our civilization. Certainly, there are parts of this "individualism" which help society prosper and grow. The ability to think out of strict group restrictions helps people achieve and create amazing things. However, in the midst of our pursuits- we have to be careful that the focus of our lives has not become reduced to selfish ambition and blind individualism.

The first step in really cultivating kindness in our lives is choosing to try to think in terms of the other. Taking times to think and empathize with other individuals. If we are not able to empathize than we are not ever going to be able to be kind people. If we cannot learn to "walk in the shoes of another" it will be impossible to seek the good of the other. To some, empathy is natural, while it may be more difficult for other people. For those with whom empathy is not easy, perhaps a simply psychological activity could go a long way. Right now, close your eyes and think of someone in your life who is going through a rough time- it could be because of a sickness, financial problem, family or relational issues, etc. Now picture this person in your mind, see them, and imagine their thoughts, fears, sorrows, hopes, and dreams. Perhaps this may feel strange or even intrusive at first, but I guarantee as you continue with this visualization, you will start thinking outside of yourself and experiencing life from the other individual's perspective. This, in turn, will help soften your being, as you turn your focus away from yourself.

Another practice you can do is just start focusing your thoughts and prayers on the other individual. One way I like to do this is put on some calming music, close my eyes, and simply bring individuals to the forefront of my mind. As I am slowly breathing in and out, I simply wish blessing, peace, and grace on them. I find through this experience, that I grow more empathetic towards these individuals, and actually, grow in my kindness towards them. For example, if I am visualizing a family member I have not talked to in a while, I feel more compelled to call them and see how there is life going. Perhaps, if it is a friend that I know is having a hard time, I see a new perspective on how I could be a blessing to them. You can also practice doing this with basic yoga positions. Perhaps, our prayers and wishes for others have less to do with them being directly blessed from God and more to do with God changing us so that we can become more of a blessing to them. To become kind people, we have to change our whole way of viewing the world and remove the narcissistic perspective by seeing life from a different point of view

Accept them for who they are

To empathize with your partner starts with loving them and accepting them as they are despite their flaws and things that annoy you. This is what it means to love and accept someone. When you do this, it is easier to take on board what they are saying and to try and see things from how they are experiencing them. Unconditional love is probably the most valued of all the types of love as it requires you to love your partner despite their failings and faults. People crave to be loved as they are.

Talk through things with them

To empathize with your partner is the capability to share in the feelings and emotions that they have. Talk and listen to them, taking the time to take in what they are saying and respond positively and actively. Give them time and space to share what is going on and cut out any distractions making them your absolute focus, and so you can listen attentively to them. This will mean so much to your partner that you care enough to give your whole attention to them. Listening to your partner in this way is one of the key things that enhances a relationship for the better.

Put yourself in their shoes

Try and think what they are going through, imagine what you would do in their circumstances and think about how you would act if you were in their shoes. Try not to give advice but have the priority of being a listening ear first and foremost. Advise if they ask for it though in a kind and sensitive manner and look to be attentive to them as much as possible. Spend time listening to what they are going through and look to be as encouraging as you can in as positive a way as possible.

How to Empathize with Others in 3 Simple Steps

Some people are natural born empathizers. But if you're not, and you want to know how to empathize with others, then this article will put you on the right track.

If you want to learn how to identify with what other people are feeling, then follow these three simple steps on how to empathize with others:

Step 1: Look Inside Yourself.

To be able to successfully empathize with another person, you need to look inside yourself and dig up that old trunk of emotions. No matter how cold-hearted someone may be, there is a small part in each of us that still understands basic human emotion.

This is easy for others, but might be a little confusing for those who have locked their feelings away. If you belong to the latter, then this might be a meaningful experience for you too.

Stop distracting yourself from your emotions and face them head-on. This enables you to have a deeper understanding of yourself as well as of others.

Step 2: Listen To What They're Not Saying.

Feelings are tricky, and people don't always mean what they say. If you want to know how to empathize with others, be a good listener.

Don't just listen to the words that are coming out of their mouth; be observant of non-verbal expressions as well.

Are their eyes tearing up even when they say they don't care? Are they fidgety even if they claim that they're not worried? These things alone can help you identify with what's going on in their hearts.

Step 3: It's Not About You.

While understanding your own emotions is a part of learning how to empathize with others, it's not all about you.

Don't go on a tirade of how you felt this and that. Be sensitive to what the other person is feeling and allow said person to express himself.

Don't butt in or make assumptions. Instead, focus your attention on the who, why, what, where and how of that other person's feelings. It's tempting to steal the limelight; but if you do so, you will have failed your basic mission.

Learning how to empathize with others is very important because it allows you to make better and informed decisions. It gives you an in-depth perspective of why people are the way they are.

The Power of Empathic Listening

Empathic Listening can be a powerful tool to build trust and rapport with those in your care. By listening to individuals, you demonstrate your commitment to them and communicate the message that they are people of value and worth. Empathic Listening can also help you positively influence the behavioural choices of the individuals in your care.

The process of Empathic Listening is not automatic. Being a good listener is a skill that takes time and effort to develop.

The Benefits of Empathic Listening

Empathic Listening is an approach to listening that allows an individual to talk through a problem and feel understood. It has some benefits.

It takes the burden off of you. You don't need to have answers or provide advice, which can sometimes be interpreted as a lecture. Also, when you listen to empathically, you don't tell the person what to do.

You can uncover the real issues. The person you are talking with is the one who leads the conversation, not you. You will gain insight into his issues without the need for prying questions.

It allows the other person to vent. The other individual can release his feelings without having to hear advice or be judged by his behaviour.

It's an excellent tool to let someone know you understand his concern. The need to feel understood is important to us all.

Five Steps to Empathic Listening

There are five key points to listening emphatically.

Give the person your undivided attention. Move away from distractions and focus your attention on the other person. Don't try and do two things at once. Make sure your nonverbal communication sends the message that you are ready to listen. Make eye contact, lean slightly forward, and nod your head periodically to let the person know you understand what he is saying.

Be nonjudgmental. If you lecture or make statements that trivialize someone's problems, it can drive him away.

Focus on feelings, not just facts. Listen carefully to understand the person's message. Some individuals can describe their problems but have a hard time identifying their feelings.

Allow silence for reflection. Before you speak, allow the other person time to reflect on what he said. Often, he will be the first one to break the silence with further information.

Use restatement to clarify messages. Put the words the person has said into your own and restated them back to him. Allow the individual to clarify your interpretation. By offering your interpretation, you give the person the opportunity to clarify and possibly expand his message.

Learn to Develop Empathic Listening

Empathic listening is also called reflective listening or active listening. This is a way of listening and then responding, in a way that will improve trust and understanding. It is an essential skill for people in disputes, and also in listening to people, we are trying to understand. This type of listening allows you to receive and interpret correctly the message the speaker is trying to impart, and then give him a response that is appropriate. The response is an important and integral facet of the listening process. It can be critical to the positive outcome of any mediation or negotiation.

Empathic listening can list among its benefits building respect and trust, and enabling you and the speaker to release your emotions. It can also reduce tension, encourage information surfacing, and create an environment that is well able to help everyone in problem-solving. This type of listening is quite useful for anyone that is involved in a conflict, and your ability to listen can set you apart from others as a strong listener and a good problem solver.

The proper use of a listening process can profoundly impact the parties involved. Especially useful in conflicts, if you utilize empathic listening, you will be judged as a helpful mediator. When you appear to be the only person who cares about what is being said, you become more credible.

Understanding what is being said in conversation, lectures or discussions is of limited use unless you can let the others involved know that you understand what is being talked about. You will not win respect and confidence in mediation until the participants realize that you understand the problem. Sometimes, if the subject is emotionally charged, empathic listening is needed to remain objective and hear all sides of the discussion.

Empathy is defined as the ability to put yourself within another person's personality so that you can understand their feelings and emotions. You let the speaker know, through empathic listening, that you understand what they're talking about, and that you don't judge them. As a listener, you need to convey this message through non-verbal ways, which include your body language. By doing this, you encourage the speaker to express whatever he wants to say without fear of being interrupted or criticized. You don't need to agree with the speaker to utilize empathic listening, but standard feedback phrases such as "I see" and "I understand" let them know that you are listening to what they're saying without judging them.

Listening with empathy is a skill that can strengthen relationships as well as your ability to assist in disputes, and contribute to discussions. It can help to strengthen your effectiveness in both your personal and professional life. Skilled listening can increase your effectiveness, and can demonstrate your willingness to let the other parties discuss while you listen.

Empathic Shielding

You know you're empathic if you find yourself picking up other people's issues. When they're sad, you're sad, when they're happy, you're happy, when they're in pain, so are you. Sorting out your issues from theirs can be very confusing and makes living life as an empath rather challenging. I would like to offer a very useful and effective technique I intuitively discovered many years ago to block out all those invading energies. Though I am empathic myself, I have developed the ability to choose to experience the energies of others or not.

Empaths naturally fluctuate their energetic vibrations to match those of other people. When someone is sad, angry, hurt, or happy, you match your energy to theirs to feel what they're feeling. Very often, this is done as an attempt to take away that person's pain; to carry their burden for them. Sometimes it stems from a belief that to understand a person's pain, you must experience it. Whatever the reason, however, a very important lesson all empaths must learn is that it is not necessary to feel or experience another's pain to ease it.

How can you stop matching the energies of those around you? By using the principle of entrainment. Entrainment is defined as the tendency for two vibrating bodies to lock into phase and vibrate in harmony; also, as the synchronization of two or more rhythmic cycles. This principle is universal and can be seen in many everyday situations. For example, two beating heart muscle cells will, in time, synchronize. The pendulums of grandfather clocks lined against a wall will begin to swing together. Women who live together for more than a month will have their menstrual cycles at the same time frame. A guitar string tuned to a particular note, when plucked, will cause another guitar string, tuned to the same note but held a distance away, to vibrate.

We can also see examples of this in emotions. Have you ever been around someone who was in a really good mood and you found yourself feeling good as well? Or how about the opposite where you were around someone who was sad or angry, and you started feeling the same way. We tend to refer to this as "infectious".

Well, you can use this same "infectious" energy to help keep you from picking up everyone else's issues. If you keep your energies higher than those of the people around you, you will find that you aren't dipping down to pick up the sadness, anger, pain, frustration, etc. You will notice that, if you spend enough time around these individuals, they will begin to match your energy and feel better! So how can you keep your energies high? By doing everything you can to stay in a good, upbeat, happy mood when someone with lower energy is near. Think of someone or something you love, count your blessings, imagine holding a kitten or a puppy or a baby, or just realize that the best thing you can do for that person is to keep your energies high instead of dropping them down to their level. Misery might love company but it isn't very helpful to have a room full of miserable people. Be the beacon, the shining light during the storm, and help raise that person's spirits. You'll both feel much, much better and you'll begin to learn that meeting a person at the level of their pain isn't the best way to help them through it.

CHAPTER 4

GUIDE ON HOW TO OVERCOME FEAR

Fear Factor

What is Fear?

So you've analyzed your ambitions and have determined the life you want to have. You can envision it, but something seems to get in the way. Could it be fear?

Fear has a way of injecting psychological toxins into our subconscious that acts like a handcuff, restraining our ability to achieve our goals. Although the fear may be perceived, it seems so real. This perceived fear plays games with our minds, robbing us of any rational thoughts we need to cherish to move ahead.

When fear is perceived, the portion of the brain involved in fear automatically reacts. It triggers behaviours such as a racing heart, anxiety, or sweaty palms. If the fear is related to doubts about your ability, the fear will allow you to come up with an excuse why you cannot accomplish your task.

The process of fear is entirely subconscious. You are driven to think, belief, and act based upon the fear you initially perceived. If the perceived fear is funnelled through unfavourable past experiences, the subconscious mind injects even more doubt, and eventually, you feel immobile, paralyzed, unable to make it past the first step.

Because we as humans do everything to avoid pain or discomfort in our lives, we give in to the fears we are fed by our subconscious. This fear prevents you from even attempting the first move. There may be times that your ambition pulsates within you and motivates you to get it past the first step, but the discomforts and doubts created by fear can be so much more powerful than your ambitions that you cannot follow through.

Over time, this fear eats away at your self-confidence. You begin to come up with excuses why things can't get done. You play the victim role. You feel sorry for yourself. You become depressed. Your self-esteem takes a plunge - all in the name of fear.

Fear Destroys Self Confidence

Ever notice that you have no problems coming up with great, profitable ideas? You are convinced that this is the big one, the idea of all ideas. The moment you conceive your idea, the level of excitement surges within you. You can't wait to share it with your friends and family. But as the days go by the enthusiasm tapers off.

Unfortunately, this is idea number 49. The people in your life have heard it so many times that they just listen to your hype to be polite. You begin to develop a reputation for "all talk and no action". Your self-confidence slowly becomes eroded. How many times has this happened to you? What do you think contributes to this syndrome? Could it be fear?

To make the bridge from ambition to achieving your plans, you must deal with the fear factor in your life. You may feel fearless in other areas of life, but in this area of goal attainment, there is something sabotaging you every time. That something is fear.

When fear intercepts your plan, your ability to execute is jeopardized. Your enthusiasm eventually disappears, and everything is at a standstill. You once again feel disappointment in yourself, wondering what happened. You level of confidence takes a serious plunge. You withdraw for the embarrassment you feel. Your self-esteem bottoms out. You remain in hibernation until you once again feel comfortable to emerge, hoping that no one remembers to ask about your once again failed project.

Fear of Success

Once fear is allowed to erode your self-confidence it remains in control of your life, lurking within the subconscious. Each failed attempt, or each time something is avoided due to fear, this fearful behaviour is reinforced even more. That fear is then transferred to all areas of your life. The erosion of your self-confidence simultaneously affects your self-esteem. The self-critic dominates your thought process, and self-doubt inevitably moves in as one begins to experience what many terms "fear of success". If the fear is not addressed, it continues to sabotage your every move.

Let's examine the real meaning of fear of success.

Your perception of self undergoes a transformation. You believe you are unworthy of any positive outcomes or recognition you will receive as a result of your achievements, so why even try?

You feel afraid of failing or making mistakes that you refuse to even make the first attempt.

Because your self-confidence is undermined you doubt your own abilities to execute a task. There is very little effort made to attempt a project.

You compare yourself with others and feel inferior, believing that no matter how much success you achieve, it will never stack up.

You begin to rationalize that even though you achieve all your goals, you still won't be able to find happiness and true contentment in your life. So what's the point?

Does any one of these apply to you? Try to examine your fears to determine if you fall into the above category.

Fear Conditioning

Fear is a normal, innate survival tool we all possess. It serves as a means of protecting us from harm. However, that same fear that protects us can also hinder our progress in life.

Let is examine what causes fear of success or any forms of fear that tend to hold us back.

The fear many of you experience that holds you back may be triggered by our culture, social structure, and values. Modern culture defines success in terms of wealth, fame, or prestige. We are compared to these norms and judged accordingly. If your level of confidence in your abilities are not sufficiently developed to feel comparatively capable a feeling of fear takes over. This results in anxiety. Here is where the conditioning begins. Over time, as this fear is experienced, this learned behaviour becomes ingrained in the psyche.

This form of fear conditioning allows you to become very intimidated. It causes you to put off doing something of great importance that can benefit your life in significant ways. Each time it gets put off the fear is reinforced even more, and the conditioning continues. Because fear is an automatic, physiological reaction, you find yourself doing or acting in ways that are so unlike you.

Fear conditioning destroys your self-image. It places you under enormous stress because you feel you cannot live up to your expectations or even worse the increased expectations that are dictated by our culture.

Overcoming Fear, Fear Not!

You are now aware of the power fear can have over you. You may have attributed your inability to gain your success momentum to fear. You must learn to overcome fear and discard this albatross that sabotages your ability to achieve your goals. But how?

You must first make that decision for CHANGE. You must choose whether to allow your fears to ruin any plans you have for the future or to break free of them. It is a choice, yes a choice you must make. Spend some time alone to look way down into the recesses of your heart and decide what fears are holding you back. Make a list of them. You are the only one who truly knows the fear that binds you. You are the only one who can free yourself from your fear. Decide to let go of the victim role that fear has you living in and make an effort to let it disappear from your life. This is the first step towards overcoming fear.

The next step to overcoming fear is awareness. Be able to recognize when fear has control of you and assess that fear. Acknowledge it out loud and ask "what am I afraid would happen to me"? What do I have to lose for trying? What am I really afraid of? Write them down. Stop and try to imagine how your life would be if you resisted the fear. Think about how great it would feel. Think about the opportunities missed by allowing the fear to stay in control.

Now that you know what you are truly afraid of try to address the fears. If it is lack of knowledge, find ways to educate yourself about the subject matter. Take a course, research on the web, find a mentor, a life coach. Associate with people who will encourage and guide you. Address all the reasons why you feel fearful and diffuse fear. As you gain more knowledge, your level of confidence will grow simultaneously. High self-confidence will replace doubts and fear.

Positive self-talk is another way to reinforce confidence and diminish fear. Giving positive self-affirmations is a form of self-conditioning that replaces the doubts lodged in the subconscious. Remind yourself that "you can" achieve.

Alternative tools for dealing with the anxiety caused by fear are neurofeedback and biofeedback therapies. These modalities help to reduce the effects of fear conditioning, restore clearer objectives, and create more focus on the goals at hand. To this end, the individual can progress at a faster pace.

Most importantly, take action. Don't just sit around hoping, thinking and planning forever, or waiting for the right time to act. The best time to start is today. Jump in! Figure out what you're good at and make that move right now. The best way to overcome fear is by being proactive. With each effort your level of confidence increases.

Above all, believe through faith that you can overcome your fears and achieve your goals. Believe that you can accomplish great things in your life.

Remember having fears is a normal part of what makes us human. It is an emotion just like love, happiness, or sadness. The problem arises when fear has so much control over your life that it hinders your ability to succeed in achieving your goals. The most successful people have fears. They just NEVER let their fears hold them back. So how badly do you want to overcome your fears? That is the question of significance.

Overcome Fear and Overcome Your Fate

Is "Fate" your genetic blueprint? A "habit pattern" you attract into your life without realizing it?

Overcoming fear is a "one quick step" process: Stop it! Fear is an emotional rush, limbic brain response to perceived danger...real or not. It's of no benefit.

"The only thing we have to fear is fear itself- nameless, unreasoning, unjustified terror which paralyzes needed efforts to convert retreat into advance." Franklin D. Roosevelt

You cannot get rid of fear - but you can create a "NO" habit response that turns your attention to solutions and inspiration. Repeat that - and you open the door to your "destiny" and leave your old genetic "fate" behind.

Do you have to overcome fear?

Nope. Many motivate themselves with fear - especially recently. The past eight years were guided by a paranoid government. Fear motivates - has for centuries. Notice the mayhem? Death, wars, destruction? Pretty hard to miss, isn't it? Now it's also in the economic arena - worldwide. Had enough? You can stop it.

Lives dominated by a fear mirror that paranoid pattern. Constantly "putting out fires, fighting to survive." Attack and counter-attack. What fun in the sports arena. Not in life.

"Anxiety is a thin stream of fear trickling through the mind. If encouraged, it cuts a channel into which all other thoughts are drained." Arthur Somers Roche

Leaders take Big Risks, and the results are magnified in full public view.

Many leaders earning millions are driven by fear. Here's an interesting comment from a businessman. "How do you explain the success of Grove, the Intel CEO, who wrote, "Only the Paranoid Survive?" He was scared all the time. I am not very different."

Many see life through the eyes of "fear." Leaders are out in life in a Big Way. Trial and error is the path to success. But errors are amplified and affect many lives. As a leader's anxiety increases so do fear. Fear clouds thinking and make a bad situation worse. That's how fear "makes itself real", and paranoia is soon justified.

How "successful" is it to put out the fires you attract or ignite? Is this success? The fear is not a conscious choice. It's there in most everyone. Fear keeps many from even attempting leadership - or seeking fame and fortune.

Fear is a poor guide to success.

How successful has fear guided our nation? Companies? Economy? You? Fear is limiting you in the same ways.

Why not try something else? Pain, strife, stress, loss, war - aren't that much fun.

"Insanity: doing the same thing over and over again and expecting different results." Albert Einstein

Fear attracts itself (fear loss - and you lose; fear attack -- you attract it.) You find what you look for - and your "experience" then validates the fear. Once caught up in that drama - it's difficult to see the alternative.

Know why? The alternative is overcoming fear: stopping it and refusing to get sucked into the limbic brain "fight or flight" response. It's a choice to stay mindful and find solutions instead. Next, you need a plan or vision of where you want to be - and you can train yourself to Focus on that instead.

Inspiration leading to solutions is a choice.

Everything you sense is vibration - and vibration exerts a "pull" like a magnet. Like energy attracts. Inspiration...with your Focus on your Vision or goal -- leads to solutions. That vision feels good - and so does pursue it. That's out of the range of the vibration of "fear." From the higher frequencies of "expecting" things to work out - they do. That's Law of Attraction in action.

The successful look for solutions and find them - sometimes with spectacular results. Fear is woven into the fabric of life. Many success stories reflect the constant struggle with fear...wins and losses...struggle and gain. That's the result of not overcoming fear, and instead of dancing with it.

Overcoming Fear.

Fear surfaces for everyone - you cannot get rid of fear (it's only a concept - a collection of thoughts. Like the number 3, you can't get rid of "3.") You can opt out, see fear as "the problem" and solve it. You can transform it by adding more to the old idea until it becomes a new idea - that's a habit too. Hard to believe? Only because you're in the "fear habit." Look beyond the familiar. You cannot solve your problems at the same level of fear that created them.

"I am an old man and have known a great many troubles, but most of them never happened." Mark Twain

Where does all the fear come from?

Your ancestors. Fear of failure and "bondage" are huge genetic patterns that interfere with creativity and success. Everyone's ancestors spent some time under the rule of a petty tyrant - either as a wife (50% of all genetic codes) or slave or servant or military. All ancestors failed many times - often with much pain and suffering. That fear is a part of your genetic blueprint. You can change it.

Not getting the success you want?

The only thing between where you are now and what you want -- is FEAR. Your genetic patterns limit you - nothing else - but an old habit. Some call that "fate". Now you know better.

What you have in your life is a reflection of your genetic blueprint - or your fate. That pattern in your subconscious built your experiences. Over many years you have modified and expanded it. You can change your fate. Is it time to change it again.

If you do not have the success you want - it is time for allowing more expansion - The fear of change and loss - can change too.

"Sure I am this day we are masters of our fate, that the task which has been set before us is not above our strength; that its pangs and toils are not beyond our endurance. As long as we have faith in our cause and an unconquerable will to win, victory will not be denied us."

Winston Churchill - Living with fear is living in chaos soup.

If you don't overcome fear - you continue to fight yourself, live in paranoia and stress - and eventually the fear wins out - and you get what you fear, along with whatever success you can hold onto. Ugh! Time to give that up. Life can be easy and fun - and successful. You need only choose it, act on the choice and live your Vision. If you're annoyed that it sounds too simple to be true - you're waking up.

Contraction and expansion is a natural creative process.

You have now outgrown your old habits of thought (and fears) and that is all that is limiting your expansion. How do you know? You want more. You feel limited, blocked and not much you try works well. Compared to where you want to be, you feel "contracted, boxed in and restricted."

When you feel you are not getting what you want and don't know how to get it: that feeling is what is keeping you stuck where you are. "Conflict" is the clash between vibrating or signalling what you want and your fear about it. Those double feelings are also called "stress".

Free yourself quickly. Simply see that you are only limiting yourself with unconscious fears. You are attracting the "fate" you fear when you allow fear to run rampant in your mind.

Get off of what is not working.

Give up hard work and action until you create a more expanded self-image - and feeling - you can't push through a genetic fear - and that's what is stopping your progress. You want what you want - and you fear (unconscious) what will happen to you if you get it. Overcome Fear Fast (at the end) can break you free of the bad habit.

"Every individual act and suffers by his peculiar teleology, which has all the inevitability of fate, so long as he does not understand it." Alfred Adler

How do you know if it is fear stopping you?

Is fear active in your life? Do you feel uneasy about being out in the world in a bigger way? Being more - expanding - new experiences - taking a chance -- new learning - giving up what you thought you wanted...looking for a new way to be and live?

Does changing your life routines, patterns, habits (friends, work, food, lifestyle) feel uneasy? It should - you have moved on and expanded - yet can't see how to get where you want to be.

Your fear is clouding your vision and inter-fear-ing with your Inspiration.

You overcome fear when you see fear as "the habit" that is attracting to you the very thing you fear. It might be the fear "I can't get what I want or what I want is outside my 'safe zone'. That's a genetic fear - it's not about now, not true, and it's not for the reasons you think.

How do you know? Listen to your self-talk. Fear masks as "avoidance" too. Thoughts such as, "I don't care about money"; If the Universe wants me to have....; I prefer "behind the scenes;" I'm not seeking fame, or anything...just a little more cash..."

"Public opinion is a weak tyrant, compared with our private opinion - what a man thinks of himself, that is which determines, or rather indicates his fate" - Henry David Thoreau.

You are changing a habit, changing your fate.

The fear of "breaking free" was formed over centuries of many deaths and much pain and suffering. You can get over it by seeing it for what it is, and talking yourself into your "now" where you are safe, and those fears are no longer justified.

You can't get rid of anything - but you can transform it into something else. Bridge from the fear - to success "in a big way" - and it will be yours. When you stop the fear - you need a "bridge of thoughts" to walk yourself to your Vision (goal) of what you want. You must have a "destination" to shift the feelings and your point of attraction from fear to solutions.

How do you know it's working? You feel hopeful and begin to expect the new success you want. Your feelings (and point of attraction) shifted from doubt to expectation.

You always get what you expect. No exceptions. Use that fact to accurately gauge where you are - then you can get to feeling what you want.

Once you have removed or softened the barrier - your inspiration guides you to new opportunities. Test the new options compared to your Vision: If they match take action - if not, wait for the choices that feel good and match your Vision.

Make it easy and make it fun.

Spend time in nature - clear your mind, open your heart, mind and body and ask questions. Seek solutions and follow your Inspiration. You can do this.

Controlling Your Mind: How to Overcome Fear

Some fears are reasonable and helpful. Other fears are unreasonable and harmful. First, one must understand the difference and, second, one must learn how to banish those that are irrational. Here are seven guidelines.

How To Overcome Fear, Guideline One: It is reasonable and helpful to have a healthy fear of things like fire, tornadoes, falling out a window, sharp objects, thieves with weapons, and so on. When fears merely guide us to be careful, they serve a positive, protective function. Any fear that becomes debilitating, however, needs fixing. If one panics in the presence of a knife, open window, or flame on a kitchen stove, even those normal fears have become too extreme. How can you overcome these hurtful and limiting fears?

How To Overcome Fear, Guideline Two: Understand the source of irrational fears. They reside in the subconscious or Deep Mind. We aren't aware of its activities. It acts not by logic but by correlation - if A occurs before B then A probably caused B. Occasionally that is true. Often it isn't. The Deep Mind can't tell the difference; in fact, it is fully unconcerned about how logical a connection may be.

How To Overcome Fear, Guideline Three: When some hurtful or unpleasant occurrence takes place after a particular event or in the presence of some person, object, or place, the Deep Mind is likely to form a correlation. When that setting event occurs again the subconscious must send your conscious mind a message (called a directive) to become fearful. Perhaps a child gets startled or pummeled by a dog and understandably becomes upset. The Deep Mind may establish a correlation between dogs in general and the need to be afraid. When that happens (and sometimes for the rest of one's life) that child will feel great fear in the presence of dogs.

How To Overcome Fear, Guideline Four: The subconscious mind is so powerful that when it sends a directive, we have to act according to it. For instance, when the Deep Mind has created and held a fear directive, we will continue to experience fear in whatever context the correlation reflects. To get rid of a fear one needs to get rid of that specific fear directive. That may take specialized training from a professional, but there are some things you can try first.

How To Overcome Fear, Guideline Five: There is a process called Gradual Accommodation that often helps. You set up situations in which you begin experiencing the problem (fear producing) stimulus from a distance such that the event (or person, etc.) does not produce fear. For example, perhaps you watch dogs in a park while you are safely secured inside your car. The process involves gradually confronting the object of fear in tiny steps. You might take a second step as simple as watching those dogs with the car window opened, then the door opened, then standing alongside the car, then sitting on a nearby bench and so on. Don't move on to the next step until you feel no fear. Your eventual goal will, perhaps, be to be able to pet a dog. Gradually you accommodate to the fear-producing object. Be patient.

How To Overcome Fear, Guideline Six: Another approach could be called the Face Down. You just swallow hard and expose yourself to the feared object or person or situation. Find a dog known to be gentle, for example. Approach it, watch it, touch it, pet it, sit and hold it. The fear will initially well up inside you. In this process, the idea is to feel the fear left as you come to understand the situation no longer requires you to be fearful. (Not suggested for children.)

How To Overcome Fear, Guideline Seven: There are counselling methods that teach one how to overcome fear in short order and which have long-lasting effects. The typical talk therapies have a very poor track record when it comes to helping people quickly and permanently learn how to overcome fear. The so-called conditioning or desensitization therapies work best.

A Guide to Overcoming Stress, Anxiety and Depression

Scientific research is now validating that stress has a considerable influence on our body's physiology, contributing to many acute and chronic illnesses. A report by the World Bank stated that 1 in 5 people suffer from depression or anxiety. Typical stresses that may be encountered in daily life include physical, chemical, infectious and psychological stresses.

The stress cycle involves our thoughts, emotions, the chemical reactions in our brain, our body and the physical sensations we feel as a result of these. Once this process begins it snowballs, gains momentum and life may feel out of control. The first stage, our thoughts is the most powerful as it is not the event that causes us stress, but the way we react to it. Thoughts start in the cortex of the brain and move quickly to the limbic system or midbrain where our emotions lie. Negative thoughts trigger an immediate emotional response such as anger, fear, hatred, grief, regret, anxiety, sadness, embarrassment or jealousy. These thoughts stimulate our nervous and hormonal systems to release stress hormones, most notably adrenaline and cortisol from our adrenal glands (kidney bean shaped glands which sit above our kidneys). In response, chemicals are released throughout the body which reaches the pituitary gland in the brain and stimulates the release of more hormones and stress chemicals. The final stage of the stress cycle is activated as these chemicals alert every organ in the body to work faster. This results in symptoms such as sweating, tremor, anxiety, churning stomach, reduced salivation, dry mouth, increased muscular activity and hyperventilation, irregular heartbeat (palpitations), chest pain, visual disturbances and tingling and numbness, as well as muscle tremors, exhaustion, general weakness and sleep disturbances.

Once upon a time, it was very beneficial for the human body to undergo these physical changes, as the main emotion experienced by our ancestors was fear triggered by an attack from a wild animal. The stress chemicals released during the attack enabled the early humans to push their bodies to the necessary extremes and escape the attack. In the 21st century, however, more complex stress emotions are triggered far more often, and they don't necessarily require a physical reaction. As a result, this continual stress response starts to wear out the body - the overproduction of stress chemicals and hormones eventually take its toll on the body and may eventually lead to cell death. Cortisol one of the predominant hormones released by the adrenal glands in response to stress produces many of the adverse effects of long-term stress. This includes depletion of DHEA, a hormone which is important for the manufacture of sex hormones such as estrogen and testosterone; an antidepressant and our so-called anti-ageing hormone. A reduction in DHEA produces symptoms of fatigue, hormonal imbalance, depression and general unwellness. Consistently elevated cortisol levels may also lead to a reduction in serotonin neurotransmission. Serotonin is a neurotransmitter which is required for a healthy mood. Low serotonin transmission is a major defect in depression.

Stress Lowers Immunity

Immune system function is also adversely affected by excess cortisol leading to depression of antibacterial, antiviral defence and increasing our allergy response. This may result in symptoms such as frequent colds and flu, cold sores, hay fever, asthma, sinusitis, migraines, and food intolerances.

Stress Increases Toxins

Stress also has significant effects on toxicity. The intestinal barrier function is a major defence against an immense load of disease-causing microorganisms from ingested food, resident bacteria, invading viruses and other insults. Psychological stress has been demonstrated to disrupt intestinal permeability. Acute stressful events are closely associated with inflammation of the colon; cells of the mucous membranes of the colon have been shown to produce elevated levels of inflammatory substances such as prostaglandin 2 and cyclooxygenase 2. This situation not only increases bacterial adherence to the intestinal lining but also reduces the secretion of important immune system compounds such as immunoglobulin A. This may lead to a condition called leaky gut, whereby improperly digested food particles and other matter leaks into circulation leading to immune activation with subsequent enhanced stress response. Certain foods in particular seem to provoke this response, including wheat, dairy and yeasts. Symptoms of leaky gut include low appetite, bloating, flatulence, abdominal pain and cramping, irregular bowel movements, as well as sinus, headaches and skin rashes.

What Can You Do?

Fortunately, there is an abundance of treatment options for stress, anxiety and depression. If the symptoms are severe or have been persisting for a considerable length of time, it may be useful to combine several approaches as outlined below:

Herbal Medicine

Herbal medicines may be very beneficial for the treatment of stress, anxiety and depression. Many clinical trials have found herbs such as St Johns Wort to be as effective as pharmaceutical anti-depressants in treating mild to moderate depression. Other herbs which are useful for alleviating symptoms of stress, anxiety and depression, include Oats, Lemon Balm, Skullcap, Zizyphus, Passionflower, Verbena and Chamomile. Another class of herbs which assists our bodies to cope with stress are the adaptogens. These include the ginsengs, such as Panax or Korean Ginseng, Siberian Ginseng, American Ginseng and Indian Ginseng also known as Ashwagandha or Withania. Other important adaptogens include Rhodiola, Schisandra, Codonopsis and Gotu Kola. Since herbs are powerful medicines, it is best to consult a professional naturopath or herbalist who can prescribe an individual prescription containing a combination of herbs specific for your needs.

Supplements

Nutritional supplements may also be of benefit in times of increased stress since increased physical, emotional and mental demands increase our demand for certain vitamins and minerals, most notably:

• Magnesium required for muscle relaxation, energy production, hormone production and healthy heart function. Magnesium deficiency is a very common occurrence. Symptoms of deficiency include muscle cramps, headaches, neck and shoulder tension, premenstrual tension, period pain and low energy. Dietary sources of magnesium include: nuts and green leafy vegetables;

• B vitamins required for healthy nervous system function, hormone and neurotransmitter, production and energy production. As B vitamins are water soluble, they are easily removed from the diet. Consuming excessive amounts of diuretics such as tea, coffee and cola drinks as well as certain medications will promote their removal from the body. Good dietary sources include: whole grains, such as oats and brewer's yeast;

• Vitamin C is important for many functions in the body, including immune system function and adrenal gland function. It is also an important antioxidant and is required for collagen production;

• Essential fatty acids such as fish oil and evening primrose oil. These are essential for healthy brain function and are often deficient in the diet. Good sources include oily fish such as salmon, ocean trout, snapper, wild barramundi and deep sea cod. Evening Primrose Oil is best taken as a supplement. When buying oil supplements ensure you buy ones with added antioxidants such as vitamin E as all oil supplements are prone to oxidation. Also, since many fish are contaminated with mercury and pesticides, ensure you buy fish supplements which have been tested and purified.

Dietary Recommendations

In times of stress, we often go for an afternoon coffee or a cola drink with sugary snacks such as chocolate, cakes, biscuits, doughnuts, etc., which give us comfort and a short burst of energy. Unfortunately, these may be exacerbating our anxiety and in the long term promoting weight gain and reducing our energy and immunity. As a result, these foods should be kept to a minimum. During times of acute anxiety, it is best to avoid caffeine-containing substances altogether as coffee (especially instant), chocolate, cola and tea may precipitate anxiety and panic attacks. Instead eat a diet of whole grains including oats, grain bread, nuts, seeds and vegetables, particularly leafy greens such as broccoli, bok choy, spinach and rocket. Include more good oils in the diet, including deep sea fish, nuts (almonds, walnuts, cashews), seeds (sunflower, pumpkin) and good quality proteins such as eggs, lean pasture fed red meat and antibiotic free chicken.

Lifestyle Recommendations

There are many other therapies which are useful for reducing stress, including massage, hypnotherapy and acupuncture. Listening to relaxing CDs may also be beneficial. Practices such as yoga, meditation and tai chi are also beneficial as they not only calm our body by producing "feel good" chemicals called endorphins but also improve immune system function, bone density and promote the removal of wastes from our bodies.

As a Naturopath, I am passionate about educating people regarding drug-free alternatives to pharmaceutical medications to treat their anxiety and stress. One such alternative which I am particularly excited about is Brainwave Entrainment. Brain Wave Entrainment Technology has made it possible to alter your brainwaves by using audio technologies to tune your brainwaves to specifically designed brainwave states simply by listening to a CD or MP3 recording. The entrainment process has been scientifically proven to naturally synchronize your brainwaves to the embedded carrier frequencies on the CD. I have personally used these technologies for over a decade with great success for insomnia and anxiety issues as well as for memory enhancement. For detailed information on our brainwave CDs visit our website listed below.

You should also aim to get adequate exercise such as walking, swimming, cycling, aerobics or weight training at least four times per week for at least 20 minutes. This will not only improve your fitness levels and cardiovascular function but will also increase the body's production of endorphins-chemical substances that can relieve anxiety and depression. Scientific research shows that routine exercise can positively affect mood and help with depression. As little as three hours per week of aerobic exercise can profoundly reduce the level of depression. The most important thing is that you find something you like and do it regularly.

Below is a list of additional recommendations to help reduce stress:

- Develop a positive attitude about everything you do; associate with positive attitude people

- Make time to relax. If you don't know how now's the time to learn!

- Learn proper breathing exercises (yoga, taichi)

- Cultivate a good sense of humour & laugh more...

- Listen to relaxing music

- Pamper yourself or be nice to yourself, e.g. have a massage or facial visit with friends and do things that you enjoy

- Permit yourself to stretch from time to time

- Get out of the hum-drum and do something different (a vacation, bush-walk, picnic)

- Always get proper rest

- Learn about your inner spirit, pray or meditate according to your conscience and beliefs

- If you're not enjoying yourself, ask why & do something about it - Life's too short

- Keep a diary of your feelings to monitor your progress

- Find something to appreciate about life every single day!

Face-To-Face With Your Fear and Anxiety

In many ways we may try to get rid of our fears and phobias by taking medication (or alcohol and drugs), going to psychotherapy, reciting affirmations, listening to hypnosis tapes, or by simply avoiding environments where we feel too much anxiety and worry.

But the truth is that experiencing some fear and anxiety is unavoidable, and it's a good sign of a healthy mind. Often, by acknowledging our fears (not avoiding them or suppressing them) we gain insight into areas in our life that we may need to improve upon.

Fear as a compass.

When your hand touches a hot stove, it feels pain, and that pain motivates you to move your hand away. In the same way, fear is an important signal and motivator that can help guide our behaviour.

Sean Cooper, author of "The Shyness and Social Anxiety System," describes fear as a kind of compass:

"Fear is like a compass that points you towards the life you want. All of your deepest desires are fear-ridden, from approaching someone you're attracted to, to starting a new business, to conquering your social anxieties. Whenever you feel fear, you know that you are going after what you truly want and growing as a person."

The truth is that whenever you try to make a significant change in your life, that change will usually be met with some kind of resistance or fear. This is because making changes requires that you start engaging in new and unfamiliar behaviours. And when engaging in these new behaviours, there will always be a degree of uncertainty - you've never acted in this way before, so you aren't sure exactly what the rewards or consequences will be. This uncertainty can be a huge contributor to our fear, anxiety, and worry. But we have to learn how to embrace it anyway.

Confronting your fears face-to-face is the only way to truly overcome them. Avoiding fearful situations only exacerbates the problem. But when you begin to see fear as a sign of growth and boundary-pushing - when you are willing to step outside of your "comfort zone" - then you give yourself an opportunity to learn more about yourself and improve your life in the face of those fears.

You can't get rid of these fears completely - you just have to find ways to embrace them in positive ways.

DIWA: Do It While Afraid

Fear doesn't go away by learning about it. You need to actively seek new experiences and gain confidence in facing these physical and psychological obstacles. Only by exposing yourself to these new experiences do you begin to rewire your brain and habituate to these new environments and situations.

Sean Cooper has a mantra that helps him overcome fear: "acknowledge feelings and take appropriate action."

There is no sense in suppressing or ignoring these feelings when they exist. Often the more we ignore or suppress our feelings, the bigger the feeling builds up inside of us. I like to sometimes think of our emotions as a baby throwing a temper tantrum. If you try to ignore the baby, it will only get louder and louder until it gets your attention. Our emotions work the same way - they are calling to us to get our attention.

Therefore, it's crucial to acknowledge and accept our feelings. And while doing this, we can often become more aware of what causes our emotions, what they are trying to tell us, and how we should act in response to these feelings.

7 Tips in Having the Right Mindset to Overcome Fear

Fear can hold us back from realizing our biggest dreams. You have to understand that fear and success can and will never go together, you have to let go of one, and if we don't overcome it, it would be impossible for us to achieve and succeed in reaching our dreams.

But as a person, you were born strong; you were born unafraid, you were born confident, you were born capable of achieving anything you could think of. It is important for us to understand the root of our fears so that we can eliminate it. It is usually from what we see, what we hear and failing to look beyond our fears that hold us back, to let us feel that we should be better of giving up than going for it. I for one was able to overcome my fear, and it took some time, it took a lot of obstacles that I had to overcome, but eventually, every bit of it was worth it. I was able to start my very own multi-million property business, and I want you to realize that your dreams can be achieved, it is possible, and you are a possibility.

Overcoming our fears is liberating and is setting our selves free from serving a lifetime of regrets and "what if's".

Here are my tips to help you overcome your fear and help you have the right mindset in reaching your dreams.

1. IDENTIFY THE THINGS THAT ARE HOLDING YOU BACK - You have to identify what it is that you're afraid of, are you afraid of failing? Are you afraid of letting go and being away from your loved ones? Whatever it is that you are afraid of, identify the root cause of it and from there on you have to confront them that they're not going to stop you from what you want and what you deserve. You have to look beyond your fear and see that an endless amount of possibility is out there only if you let go of your fears.

2. SELF-MOTIVATION - Self-motivation is very powerful in changing one's ability to handle and confront fears. If you are having doubts, each day writes something positive that you can repeat to yourself every morning. Write down the things you want to happen and the things you

want to accomplish each day. Make everything you write down as positive and as motivating as it can be. It will help you get through.

3. DO IT ANYWAY - Fear may stop us, either temporarily or permanently but we have to face the truth that if we do not get it over it, fear will eventually find its way back to us in other ways. The best way to overcome it is to decide that fear will not stop you. Your dreams are too important to just write them off due to fear.

4. REALIZE THAT YOU ARE A POSSIBILITY - From the moment you were born, you were already a success. You have the God-given capabilities, skills and life to do all that you can accomplish. Don't waste life by taking a step back and live it by wishing you could have done better, act now because now is the time to do better. What you dream of is POSSIBLE if you decide to make it happen.

5. BE POSITIVE AND BE WITH POSITIVE AND MOTIVATIONAL PEOPLE - One way to overcome your fear is by living day to day positively and surrounding yourself with positive thinking people who can give you the confidence, who can support and motivate you into becoming the best that you can be. Negative people will only see your weakness and bring you down. Stay away from them and be with the right group who can keep you positive.

6. DO YOUR RESEARCH - If ever you are afraid of failing, study it. Learn what you need to learn from the experts to minimize the risk of failing, to know what to do and to avoid what not to do. Learn as much as you can, keep it in heart and mind and gain as much experience, values and lessons as you can. You can even get yourself a mentor to guide you and get you through the process of living your passion.

7. PRAY AND STRENGTHEN YOUR FAITH - Fear is usually the result of weakness inside, and we can ask help by Praying to God, He will always be our stronghold, and He will always plan what is best for us. When you have God with you, nothing and nobody, not even fear can hold you back from what you are destined for.

How to Overcome Fear - 7 Tips to Help You Overcome Fear

- Public speaking
- Dogs
- Spiders
- Going somewhere new
- Ageing
- Socialising
- Losing a partner
- Starting a new job
- Trying a new activity - particularly on our own
- Moving from the area in which you live
- Flying

Do any of these things fill you with dread? Well, you're not alone!

We all feel some or all of these fears and many others to boot! Whatever our excuse for not achieving something, fear is usually involved in it somewhere.

It's not just our doubts that stop us from moving forward, very often it can be our friends and family that are very happy to give us their opinions that just pile on top of the self-doubt that we already have.

Can we live fearless lives? Actually no, but we can become far better at being able to overcome fear and thus substantially reduce it's negative effect on our lives. Some fears we need to have to alert us of danger, but it is the ones that stop us from progressing positively in life that we need to learn to put in perspective.

It's a well-known fact that most of us only achieve a small percentage of our full potential in life; wouldn't it be great to increase that potential?

From the Cradle to the Grave

One of the main problems is that we are all told from the cradle to the grave, be careful with this, don't do that it's dangerous, I wouldn't recommend that it's too risky, I don't think you'll be able to do that.

We have so much reinforced negative conditioning. We are taught to fear but rarely taught how to overcome fear. Of course I realise that when your parents advise you to pay attention when crossing the road, this is obviously sensible and is the correct advice, but when making a decision where your life is clearly not at risk, we must assess for ourselves the real risks involved.

That said, some people do have to make decisions which may result in a situation or activity where their lives could be at risk, but they still go for it anyway. If this was not the case there would be a lot of sport not played, planes not flown, wars not fought, countries not governed and challenges not taken.

Here are seven tips to help you overcome fear and grab the life you deserve:

1. The "No Lose Scenario"

When you've made changes in your life previously, what were the outcomes? In most cases, the outcomes were probably good or fairly neutral. Occasionally you may have made a decision that you now feel was wrong. But, in making what you see as a wrong decision, you learned something, so in a way, none of the decisions was wrong. Given those results, can we say there is no "wrong" decision, I think so? Also, don't forget that sometimes what you previously thought was a bad decision, may lead you to the right place in the end. Things often happen for a reason and happen when we are ready for them.

2. You Need To Make Mistakes

We are all going to make mistakes, so get used to it! We all make mistakes - all the time. If we didn't, how would we learn? Have you ever heard the saying: "There's no such thing as failure, only feedback."?

Not everything in life is explained in a textbook, and even if it were, you wouldn't remember it all anyway. We remember better when we have experienced something because we have more senses attached to that memory. If we burn ourselves on a hot pan, we will certainly remember to be more careful in future as we know what it FEELS like if we touch a pan that is very hot. Get used to mistakes, expect them and most of all learn from them!

3. The Things You Want To Do ARE Achievable

Nearly all the things that we could possibly think of doing have been done before which means they are achievable. Therefore, if it's already been done, there's a good chance that you can do it too, you just need to learn how and then do the work necessary to get you there.

4. You Will Handle It

One of things that Susan Jeffers says in her book; "Feel The Fear And Do It Anyway" is to think to yourself that whatever comes your way, you'll handle it. Think about your life, isn't that true? You have handled everything that has come your way so far, one way or another and you're surviving to tell the tale!

5. Reduce Worry And Stress

If you learn to overcome fear more effectively, you will reduce the amount that you worry. If you reduce the amount that you worry, you will reduce your levels of stress. If you reduce your levels of stress, your health will undoubtedly benefit.

6. Be Happier

Think for a moment, if you were able to substantially reduce your fear, what things would you like to do? And if you did those things, how do you think you would feel? Wouldn't your life be so much more exhilarating? So many new opportunities would be available to you. Your life would carry so many more great experiences and achievements which could only make you happier.

7. You've Already Done It

You will have made many decisions throughout your life and your life has probably changed many times, so it's a good thing to look back and say, I was scared but I went ahead anyway. Remember the sense of achievement that you felt when things went to plan or the enjoyment you felt when you tried an activity that you were scared of beforehand.

And Finally - Why Is It So Essential That You Learn To Overcome Fear?

The thing that we should fear the most is the prospect that our lives will never change, that we will never grow or learn anything else for the rest of our lives because of fear. Surely that would be the worst thing and such a waste of a life where so much is possible for us.

Learning how to overcome fear is essential for us to make our lives worth living.

Overcoming Fears with Psychic Abilities

Did You know that You have the power to overcome fear by using your psychic skills? Well, You do. By tapping into the unseen powers around and within, You can leave yourself feeling relaxed, empowered and ready to face what comes.

First of all, the root of many fears stems from worry about the future. We lose our center thinking about situations out of our control. For example, being afraid the plane will crash, a tornado will strike, or our loved ones won't arrive safely. We take ourselves out of alignment with our Higher Selves when we fear things won't work out the way we want them to. We start focusing on the worst case scenario and drain our energy. All the what ifs start to hold us in a state of fear.

Remember that when faced with actual bodily harm You can trust yourself to know what to do in a scary situation when it's right in front of You. What I'm talking about here is how to feel better in the now. You have the psychic power to release the fears holding you back and leave yourself feeling calm, centered, peaceful and confident in the now.

Here are some ideas that can help You with overcoming fears.

Trust All is Well and everything is in Divine Order. Allow yourself to know in your heart and mind that whatever comes your way, You are OK.

See and feel yourself succeeding. You can project your consciousness into the future and notice what it's like to have lived past the event that had You feeling scared. Allowing yourself to feel in the now that You made it through the hard time and you've thrived.

Take time to mediate and allow yourself to be grounded with the earth energy and connected with the cosmic energy. This will keep You in the now. In the now is where your personal power rests.

Ask your guides or angels for help. Archangel Michael's expertise is in removing fears.

Remember the law of attraction says whatever You give your attention to grows stronger. Figure out what it is You want to happen and focus on that. Or just pay attention to things in your now that you appreciate, things that make You feel good.

What if You try a bunch of techniques and You still feel afraid? Try playing the even if... game. This tool has You project yourself into your fear and You see and know you'll be OK no matter what. Even if (fill in the blank) happens, I know I'll be ok.

I've found the even if tool helpful for overcoming my fears — for example, the fear of dying while my children are young. Even if I die while they are young, I know they will be ok. Another example, worry about getting in a car accident. Even if I get into a car accident, I know I'll be ok.

Just by using the even if tool I was able to stop focusing about what I didn't want because I was able to feel in my body, heart and mind that I am OK and would be OK no matter what.

Underlying a lot of fears is the fear of dying. If You are attracted to this site, You most likely have awareness of yourself as an eternal and spiritual being. If You see death as a transition to a different realm, then there isn't really much to fear

CHAPTER 5

SURVIVAL GUIDE FOR EMPHATIC AND HIGHLY SENSITIVE PEOPLE

Emotional Intelligence and the Empathic Spirit

The mood was festive and joyful. The ambience of the large and magnificent arena concurred with the joyful energy that permeated the room. The Master of Ceremonies had prepared a first Class meeting as usual. I had noticed that the MC has a habit of doing a first class job at everything he does, this habit must have something to do with his childhood, I was thinking.

The kind Gentleman walked up to the podium and my chagrin, he told a story about a child, we were all ears. Now, I will share the story with you, as best as I can remember it.

There was a young lad in a past age, Let's call him Hans, in a country where they set buckets of water on the floor to use as fire extinguishers. Hans had been taught well by his parents; he was well versed with truth and the propriety of his society. Hans was the boy that everyone knew was going to do right all of his life. This was the boy that always had his homework done and done right. Everyone who knew him expected him to do what was right, and do it on time.

It was the beginning of a new school year, complete with all the joy, jokes, the hope of a new beginning and the nervous anticipation that goes along with such events. Everyone who had anything to do with the school was attending. Hans was sitting on the front row.

Children can get very nervous on the first day of school and this day was no different. Hans noticed the young girl on his left side. She appeared to be more than nervous and sorrowing with anxiety, shame and very troubled.

Hans walked over the hallway, picked up one of the buckets of water, walked back with everybody now watching him and poured the entire bucket on the young girl. Pandemonium erupted in the auditorium. Teachers moved to her defence and Hans was in a lot of trouble.

Hans was taken to the principal's office and was questioned there. Hans never spoke a word but rather took his punishment like a man. Nobody could get a single word of explanation from Hans, about the incident that entire year.

He held his peace. As time went on the incident began to dim in mind and memories of the students and faculty. It was now the last day of School, and his schoolmaster stopped him on his way out and asked him why he poured the bucked on the young girl.

Hans replied; "Sir, she had wet her dress. I could see that she could not take the shame. I poured water to spare her the humiliation. "But Hans, you got into a lot of trouble over that," said the schoolmaster.

Then Hans said: "I know, and I could take the punishment" "But she was not strong enough to take the humiliation".

Listening with great care as the first class speaker delivered this story, it hit me. That is the truth being taught hit me; I got it. The truth received that day was as magnificent as the expansive auditorium and as awe-striking as the joy and energy of the crowd.

The truth received, will not openly be written here because you can figure it out on your own. However, I will leave you with this statement; this is the kind of thing that God does for us.

Resources for Empaths and Emotionally Sensitive People

Empaths have a natural ability to sense not only their own but also the emotions of others. This innate skill can be observed in babies. This ability usually subsides in childhood as we learn to focus more on verbal cues than emotional ones.

But for some people, the flow of emotional information just keeps coming. This can lead to powerful internal conflicts as they pick up incoherent verbal and emotional messages from people (such as when someone lies or suppresses anger). It can also quickly become overwhelming in social settings where the sheer quantity of emotional information can be too much to handle.

Emotional Intelligence is defined as "the ability, capacity, or skill to perceive, assess, and manage the emotions of one's self, of others, and groups" (Salovey and Mayer, 1990). Developing your Emotional Intelligence means that you have tools and processes to manage these emotional data.

If you are interested in Emotional Intelligence i've wrote a good introduction book of Emotional Intelligence, the title name is "Introducing Emotional Intelligence" by the way of course by Daniel Anderson.

Are you an Empath?

- Do you feel anxious or nervous in a crowd (4+ people)?

- Does your mood vary seemingly at random (getting angry or sad for no apparent reason)

- Do you feel a change in your physical energy level when you're in a crowd (tired, wired)

- Do you have a hard time falling asleep before midnight or do you procrastinate going to bed?

- Do you have physical symptoms that related to hearing (ringing, popping, itching in the ear)?

- Do you feel emotionally uncomfortable when someone touches or is close to you?

Disclaimer: This checklist is not a diagnostic or treatment tool. Some of the characteristics of Empaths can be diagnosed as ADD, agoraphobia or clinical depression. Contact your health care professional if you have any questions, need diagnostic or treatment for a mental health issue.

Empath Resources

Fortunately, there are more and more online resources available for Empaths. Unfortunately, most of these resources suggest a process that is likely to make things worse for you! Any kind of "protective mental shield" is based on the assumption that emotional information is threatening. If you go down that path, you will have to "defend" yourself for the rest of your life. How exhausting does that sound?

My work is result-based: if it works, keep doing it! As an Empath, these are the three tools I find most effective to manage the flow of emotional information I receive constantly. Try them out and see for yourself which one works best for you.

Being Transparent:

When we feel threatened by our surroundings, we become physically tense, and our energy field (the magnetic field that wraps around our body) becomes dense and constricted.

When you notice this tension, imagine that your energy field is expanding, like a gas. The particles are getting more and more spaced out, making your energy field thinner and much bigger. As your energy field becomes looser, emotions go right through you, like a rock falling through water. Instead of being caught in your dense energy field, the emotions of others will simply flow through you.

Adjust the Volume:

Sometimes the noise from other people's emotions gets so loud that we can't hear ourselves think! We get confused, hesitant, frustrated. Close your eyes and imagine two volume dials in front of you that go from 0 to 10. One says "Me", and the other says "Everything else". Turn the "Me" dial to 10, and the "Everything else" dial to 0. Instantly, your mind will respond to this request, and the chatter will calm down.

Progressive Affirmations:

Progressive affirmations can help you build up to where you want to be. Keep in mind that affirmations must ALWAYS feel good to be effective. So start at the "easiest" affirmation and say it for a few days. When you feel ready, move on to the next level for a few days until you can say the "top" affirmation while feeling good.

"I am willing to master my Empath abilities."

"I am ready to master my Empath abilities"

"I am choosing to master my Empath abilities."

Keep in mind that practice makes perfect. Try doing it in your head before you throw yourself in a tough situation (such as the mall or a party).

Once you are comfortable managing your Empath skills, you are ready to move on and develop your Emotional Intelligence by productively using emotional data in your daily life.

4 Steps to Turn Your Sensitivity into Your Superpower

Have you ever been told you're too sensitive? Or, to grow a thicker skin? Do you have a habit of taking on other people's pain? Do you consistently put others' needs before your own? Do you struggle with your sensitivity, at any time, in any way?

If you're like me, you might be an empath, a highly-sensitive person, or maybe someone with an extra dose of sensitivity. There's a spectrum, and if you find that you have heightened sensitivity, you likely fall somewhere within the spectrum of empaths.

Although, as sensitive souls, we know how painful it can be, it's important to know that sensitivity is a source of inner power. What's tricky, is knowing how to manage sensitivity -- so that rather than disempowering us, it empowers us instead.

There's no question in my mind that sensitive people must be vigilant about self-care. Daily self-care is not an option if you want to thrive as a sensitive person. And, fortunately, with the right methods and tools, it's possible to turn your sensitivity into your superpower!

What do I mean by turning your sensitivity into your superpower? I mean nurturing your inner gifts, such as intuition, inner vision, deep knowing, psychic ability, love, compassion, healing energy, creativity, artistic vision, and so many more -- and letting them shine.

Our creative abilities come from our senses, and we help them flourish by creating a nurturing inner environment.

Here are 4 Steps to Turn Your Sensitivity into Your Superpower:

STEP 1: EMBRACE

This is where you start. Tune your awareness to what lies within you. How does sensitivity show up for you? How does it assist you? How does it hinder you? Embrace everything that shows up with love, and acceptance. Let go of judgement.

Write a list of all the things you love about your sensitivity. Write a list of all that is painful. Practice embracing yourself with love, when you notice either the pleasurable or painful aspects of your sensitivity.

For one of my clients, when she learned how to embrace her sensitivity, without making it wrong, she was able to harness it in her work as an artist. Now she infuses her sensitive gifts into her creative projects, and her work has blossomed.

STEP 2: CLEAR

This step creates space for the magical part of your sensitivity to assist you in ways you could never imagine. Freeing ourselves from judgement, other people's opinions, other people's feelings, and all the old emotions we've stuffed down is the key to allowing our sensitivity to shine.

Sensitive people are prone to experiencing intense bouts of self-doubt, anxiety, fear, sadness, and overwhelm. Also, because we are sensitive, we're sometimes more likely to accept beliefs that aren't even ours. When these emotions and beliefs get stuck in our system, they contribute to persistent limiting patterns.

Clearing out old stuck emotions, and releasing limiting beliefs and patterns is crucial for our sensitivity to thrive truly. Clearing techniques include meditation, deep breathing, yoga, EFT tapping, matrix reimprinting, heart breath, and various talk and touch therapies.

Experiment with what works for you. Many times, if not most, it's helpful to enlist professional help when dealing with old persistent patterns and stuck emotions.

And, remember, self-love is the healing elixir for clearing any, and all, old negativity.

STEP 3: RECHARGE

Cell phones, with all of their amazing apps, only work when they're charged. Think of your superpower, or your inner power, like a battery that needs recharging regularly. When we don't recharge, we lose power. Recharging is essential.

Recharging for sensitive people often means a daily self-care ritual, perhaps combined with services such as massage, sauna, salt therapy, and energy therapies.

It also means creating healthy routines to allow for alone-time, creative expression, sleep, and time in nature.

And perhaps the most important aspect of recharging is the presence of healthy boundaries. Without them, overload and burn-out are almost guaranteed. Boundaries can be firm, hard, loose, stretchy, soft, or any way you want them. However, you decide to create them, remember that boundaries are essential to protect yourself from unwanted energy, people, ideas, and anything else that's not a match for your system.

STEP 4: ACTIVATE

Once you've become clear on the different aspects of your sensitivity, you've begun to clear out old, stuck energy, and you're regularly recharging your inner power, you're ready to active your gifts. As with anything, this is a process. The more you repeat the steps in the process, the easier, and more powerful it will become.

Decide now, which of your sensitive inner gifts will you expand? Which of your natural sensitivities will help you enrich your work life? Your relationships? Your Health? Your Spiritual Life? Your creative life? How will you shine your gifts, and with whom?

When you begin to see the picture of how sensitivity can flow through your life, activate one aspect of your sensitivity. For example, if you have a lot of compassion, you might choose to volunteer as a way to share your compassion. Or, if you have a gift for sensing subtle energy, you could expand your knowledge of energy therapies. The possibilities are endless. The goal here is to expand what you already possess, in the way that enriches your life. This is what turns your sensitivity into your superpower.

Throughout the process of activating your inner gifts, it's important to recycle through the first three steps: embrace, Clear, Recharge. A continual act of self-love will help you continually activate your brilliance.

You deserve your magnificence!

Here's to Bold Sensitivity!

9 Tips for the Spiritually Sensitive and Empaths

An empath is a highly sensitive person who can feel the emotional and physical states of the people around them. This, of course, can be problematic for the individual while walking through crowds or being around people who are in a negative state of mind.

They also have the ability, if they set aside any bias or emotional attachment, to sense truth and the motives of others.

Unfortunately, there are many people who are highly empathic and don't realize it. They struggle daily with not only their emotions but those of everyone around them. Some attempt self-medication with alcohol or drugs, or are prescribed drugs, that compound the issue, by doctors who don't understand the problem.

Thankfully, if you're an empath, there are other ways to deal with it. Below are things we've learned, as empaths, that we must do if we want to feel good daily.

1) Diet is key. You must be careful about how you fuel your body. Sugar and junk food will affect how you feel more so than other people, so it's best to avoid it as much as possible. Also, go easy on fruit sugar and make sure you are getting enough quality protein (not non- fermented, processed soy).

2) Regular exercise makes everyone feel better, and it's especially important for empaths. You don't need to go to a gym to exercise, of course, and a crowded gym might not be the best place for you.

3) Make sure to schedule alone time to recharge; reading or walks in nature are two good ways. Regular solitude is a healing balm to the spiritually sensitive.

4) Be careful of who you allow in your inner circle. Don't try to save toxic people.

5) Meditate daily to clear your mind and calm your energy. There are many ways to meditate. For beginners, we recommend just sitting quietly with your eyes closed, and focusing exclusively on your breathing, a mantra, or counting from one to 500.

6) Burn white sage or use other energy clearing and protection methods to keep your space energetically clean.

7) Know that you always have access to spiritual help and protection from the other side. We call upon Arch Angel Michael for clearing and protection often, and there's no such thing as asking for too much help of him, or other helpful guides and beings of the Light, or God.

8) When you are feeling down, anxious, or otherwise negative, stop, breath, and ask yourself, "Are these feelings from me or someone else?" even if you are alone, you may be picking up other people's thoughts or energy from many miles away. You have the option to reject outside, negative energy and the right to feel good. Stand your ground and refuse to take on the energy of others. Sometimes you just have not to care.

9) Finally, you need to be aware of the information we've shared previously about spirit attachment and possession, which can be more of a problem for empaths. A weakened energy state, due to various reasons such as excess drinking, drugs, or stress, can inadvertently invite toxic energy in the form of stray souls, entities, or even demonic energy, which can greatly interfere with all areas of your life.

It isn't easy maintaining a balanced state of mind as an empath but following these tips will help you feel better. You'll also have more energy to use your empathic ability in positive ways, such as being able to understand others' perspectives acutely well, and offering guidance when appropriate.

A Survival Guide for Empaths and Highly Sensitive Persons

Empaths are very special people and face multiple daily challenges. You connect with the energy of others sharing your space, and also your environment (through energy imprints). This can be overwhelming at times, and to gain control and manage your energy, a few tools can be essential. Here are some tips and techniques that have proven to be valuable assets for the empath's toolbox.

Learn how to disengage from the energy of others. How do you accomplish this? You must first know your energy. The awareness of what is yours versus other people is key to this step. I suggest reading Yvonne Perry's book, Whose Stuff Is This? This is an excellent reference book to begin learning about energy management. Distress and relaxation space is another necessity. It can be your man cave, your reading nook, or porch swing. It just needs to be a space where you can go to have time out and be away from the energy of others so that you might centre and recharge yourself.

Positive affirmations are also very helpful. A positive affirmation is a short sentence or two that supports positive thought patterns and can re-train your brain (The Audiobooks of Anthony Proctor are a really good choice) . An example, let me receive what is in my best and highest good at this time, is both raising your energetic signature and open-ended. Why is open-ended a good thing? It doesn't define, which can sometimes place limits or expectations providing an unintended consequence. What is what is the best and highest good is better than you have imagined? If you leave it open ended, it can flow right to you. I enjoyed, Outrageous Openness by Tosha Silver, which did a wonderful job of breaking this down and giving more insight into how this works.

Shielding is another tool you can use when you are just getting started. This involves calling in a high vibrational energetic field to protect you. You can call in Angels and see them standing by you in your mind's eye, or imagining a white light encasing you. Another method is to see yourself in armour made of mirrors which send energy right back to its source. A developed empath will be able to allow energy to flow through without absorbing any. This takes confidence and skill. You can develop this with practice. It is the knowledge that any energy that flows towards you is temporary, like a breeze. It can flow right through you. You can feel it, know it does not belong to you and allow it to pass through without absorbing any of it.

Good energetic hygiene is a must for any empath. It starts with a basic understanding of chakras, and then a simple visualization of cleansing them. Some people see the chakra wheels of colour and imagine them spinning with bright, healthy colour and any dark spots of negativity are removed. Doing this in the shower can be quite effective as any negativity goes right down the drain with the dirty bath water! You can also imagine white light coming in through your crown chakra, nourishing and replenishing the chakras.

Meditation and centring are also valuable assets for your empathic toolbox. Meditation for 10-20 daily will bring profound change. Centring involves coming back to self. Empaths connect with others, and it's like an energetic handshake. Your energy goes out to meet and greet others, and centring brings you back into your body fully. This allows you to align with spirit/ source energy and step out of ego. Mindfulness is great for centring. Try to live in the moment, and whatever emotion comes up to acknowledge, express and then release it.

Stones and essential oils can also be helpful. Depending on how you are wired you might prefer one more than the other. Remember you are an individual, your expression of empathic ability and empathic experience may be similar to another person's. However, the truth is you are a unique divine expression. That means you will vibe strongly and have an affinity with some things and not others. That's your beauty and why the world needs you!

Forgiving others and forgiving self is one of the most powerful tools you have. It will clear your energy and raise your vibrational rate. Remember forgiveness is for your well-being; the other person doesn't need "to forgive you" for the benefit. It can be a challenge to do this. However, it is necessary for your growth and evolution. No one has walked this earth and not harmed, intentionally or unintentionally, another being. It is part of the human experience. So like the prayer says... forgive others and forgive yourself.

The root chakra connects us to the earth. Be aware of this and using visualization ground into the earth. See (using your mind's eye) a cord connecting you to the earth. You can then use it to send negative energy into the earth where it is absorbed and to draw up nourishing energy from the centre of the earth. Doing this will increase your energy flow.

Others helpful techniques include listening to music or nature sounds. Spending time in nature and with your pets is a great way to relax, clear your energy and centre yourself. Exercise programs will support a good energetic flow. Yoga is really good because it combines breathing with poses that encourage alignment and flow of energy.

Keep your environment clear of negativity. Raise those vibes! The Native Americans' have been smudging with great results for years. Burning sage while stating an intention is a great method for clearing energy. In your office area, you can use a spritzer bottle with water and salt, or make an aromatherapy spritzer. If you use essential oils remember that oil and water don't mix so, you'll want to add some witch hazel or alcohol to the water and oils. A cup of water, ¼ cup of witch hazel and 7-10 drops of oil. Journal the gratitude! Ending the day by writing a list of things you are grateful for in a journal and then stating an intention or affirmation keeps the positive energy flowing.

CPSIA information can be obtained
at www.ICGtesting.com
Printed in the USA
BVHW011102170521
607543BV00008B/1158

9 781667 111773